LET MY
PEOPLE
GROW

Also by Michael Harper

POWER FOR THE BODY OF CHRIST
AS AT THE BEGINNING
WALK IN THE SPIRIT
SPIRITUAL WARFARE
NONE CAN GUESS
GLORY IN THE CHURCH
A NEW WAY OF LIVING

LET MY PEOPLE GROW

Ministry and Leadership in the Church

MICHAEL HARPER

LOGOS INTERNATIONAL
PLAINFIELD, NEW JERSEY

LET MY PEOPLE GROW!
Copyright © 1977 by Michael Harper

Printed in the United States of America
Published by Logos International (Plainfield, New Jersey 07061) by special arrangement with Michael Harper, and Hodder and Stoughton Ltd. (Great Britain).
ISBN 0-88270-236-X
Library of Congress Catalog Card Number: 77-73840

To Jeanne

*Quotations from the Bible are taken from
the Revised Standard Version if no other
translation is mentioned.*

Contents

A Prologue

On the road to Bristol
A Prologue

TODAY THE MODERN M4 motorway snakes across the Berkshire Downs, skirts Swindon and strikes like a dagger into the very heart of Bristol. From London you can be in Bristol in less than two hours. But in 1746 it was a very different matter. The journey would have taken several days on horseback, and it was on one such journey that John Wesley made what to him was a momentous discovery. It was his custom to take plenty of reading matter with him to while away the tedium of the journey and to inform his mind. And it was in 1746 on the road to Bristol that Wesley read a book called *Account of the Primitive Church*. It had been written in 1691 by a Puritan called Peter King. The important thing about this incident is that this book convinced Wesley that bishops and presbyters were the same in the New Testament and that, therefore, presbyters had as much right as bishops to ordain fellow presbyters. We know (from a letter that John and his brother Charles wrote a few weeks earlier) that he had until his journey to Bristol believed strongly in the classical Anglican position of the three-fold ministry of bishops, presbyters and deacons. Peter King's book changed all that. And many years later Wesley's discovery on the Bristol road was to lead to the separation of the Methodists from the Anglican Church.

There is need for clear thinking on the ministry at the

present time. Much of it is in the melting-pot. Should the permanent diaconate be restored? Should we expect apostles today? Are bishops necessary? Should we ordain women? Where are the prophets? Is there an order of healers? Should there be a professional ministry at all? These are all questions people are asking. We are also under pressure from a new kind of independency, the "house-church movement", people who have set up new churches and ministries within them, but who want to maintain their links with other churches. The charismatic movement is challenging the Church to take seriously the "every-member ministry" of the early Church, but can that ministry be contained within the old traditional structures of the historic churches? When new life burgeons out, will it not be inhibited by the church order of a bygone age?

The charismatic movement in particular needs to heed carefully the implications of new order and ministry in the Church. Charismatics have so convinced themselves that they cannot think themselves *into* blessing, they are fearful that they will think themselves *out of* blessing. What is needed is a little less hot air, and many more cool breezes of the Spirit to chill the brain, clear away the mists of mindless uncertainties and get what Agatha Christie's little Belgian detective, Hercule Poirot, always used to call "the little grey cells" to work properly. Unfortunately it is as true in the Christian Church as it is in the field of economics that, to quote Professor J. K. Galbraith, "originality is taken to be the mask of instability". We need to be bold enough to move out into fresh pastures, whilst not being foolish enough to neglect the old paths. One only hopes that this book will not be another example of the 'bland leading the bland'.

With so many religious books being published, one needs increasingly to justify the contribution of yet another. Writers need to beware of what Juvenal called the *insanabile cacoethes scribendi* — a crazy itch to write. But this book is one which I have long wanted to write. And, since in several parts it is fairly radical in its treatment of the subject, I would not want people to jump to the wrong conclusions. First, I am *not* a disillusioned Anglican. It is only those who have illusions that can become disillusioned, and I have never had illusions about the weaknesses and imperfections of Anglicanism. I see it in need of radical and urgent reform and renewal in the area of its ministry. But I see no reason why this should not be accomplished, and I am happy to be part of the change which has for some time now been taking place. Secondly, I am *not* a clergyman with a chip on my shoulder. I count myself fortunate to have served with men like Reg Bazire, Tom Smail and John Stott, and more recently John Barter, all of whom have taught me a great deal about what Christian ministry is all about. I have had over twenty years of satisfying ministry in the Church of England. But this does not blind me to the need for changes.

It is an interesting fact that John Wesley did not act on his discovery on the Bristol road for thirty-eight years! This is in marked contrast to modern leaders who, when they make some new discovery, want the whole world to know by next Thursday morning at the latest. But in this area we have to be particularly careful to move cautiously. Even though Wesley waited so long, he did eventually in 1784 ordain Richard Whatcoat and Thomas Vasey as deacons, and the next day as presbyters. Methodism ceased to be a renewal movement. It had become a new denomination. Few people, knowing the obtuseness of the English bishops of that time, would today condemn Wesley for what he did on that occasion. The circumstances demanded it. One can only commend Wesley for his restraint for so many years. Nevertheless we need to see the dangers. God's call is the same today — 'Let my people grow' — and wherever there are barriers to this growth, the temptation will be to overthrow them. Let us learn from the past, and even if, as we shall see, the conclusions we draw from the New Testament and Church history are somewhat different from those of John Wesley, let us strive 'to maintain the unity of the Spirit in the bond of peace', remembering that, though one person plants and another waters, it is, according to Paul, *God who gives the growth.*

* * *

There are so many to whom I am indebted for their help in the writing of this book. To my fellow workers in Holy Trinity, Hounslow, for their patience and love in freeing me to write this book so soon after arriving in the parish. To Norman Lawrence and John Barter for reading the MS. for me, and, especially, to Norah Garratt who has typed it with such cheerfulness and conscientiousness, even when at times she has not been well. Her labour of love has been a real encouragement to me. I should also like to thank Debbie Taylor for her researches on my behalf at the Bodleian library in Oxford, and Pam Button for typing some of the corrections.

I am most grateful also to Canon Michael Green for kindly reading the MS. and making so many useful comments and corrections, and to the members of the National Evangelical Anglican Congress (1977) study group on the ministry, who have helped to stimulate my thinking, and particularly to Andrew Kirk for permission to quote from his study paper submitted to this group. I should also like to thank John Poulton for permission to quote from the 'Let my people grow' report, from which the title of this book is taken.

Last but not least, I want to thank my wife Jeanne to whom this book is dedicated, who is my partner in life and ministry, who has encouraged me in the writing of this book, and who was my closest partner in the difficult pioneering days of the Fountain Trust.

I am very grateful to Edward England and his staff at Hodder & Stoughton for their assistance throughout. In spite of the magnitude of their business operations they still manage to maintain the family atmosphere.

And what more appropriate day could have been found for finishing the book than Ascension Day? May the ascended Christ continue to give his gifts 'for the work of ministry...

until we all attain to the unity of the faith and of the knowledge of the Son of God to mature manhood, to the measure of the stature of the fullness of Christ'.

Michael Harper   Ascension Day 1976
Hounslow, Middlesex

1

Let My People Grow!

Two things about the Christian religion must surely be clear to anybody with eyes in his head. One is that men cannot do without it; the other, that they cannot do with it as it is. Matthew Arnold

A LOT HAS happened since Matthew Arnold wrote these words. Millions of people have made the discovery that you *can* do without Christianity, and get on quite nicely. They have not been struck down by thunderbolts from heaven. But there would still be a near unanimous voice that we really cannot go on with it as it is. We are concerned in this book with only one aspect of the Christian religion — the ministry. The situation world-wide is now so serious that some Christians regard the ministry as a disposable asset. Others would not even count it an asset. But most would agree that it is in need of a fairly radical overhaul. Everywhere there is a call for reform, reminding us of God's message to Pharaoh — 'Let my people go.'

As the Israelites in the slave-labour camps of Egypt pined for their freedom, so for some there is a nostalgic longing for the simplicity of the pristine Church. Roland Allen was a man who dreamed dreams and saw visions. He wrote in his now famous book with the intriguing title *The Spontaneous Expansion of the Church*[1]

Men say that such can only be for dreamers, that the age of that simple expansion has gone by... I must acknowledge that to sigh after an inefficient simplicity is vain, and worse than vain. But if we, toiling under the burden of our organisations, sigh for that spontaneous freedom of expanding life, it is because we see in it something divine, something in its very nature profoundly efficient, something which we would gladly recover, something which the elaboration of our modern machinery obscures and deadens and kills.

We need more such dreams, but better still the reality of them.

A deep malaise has settled on our churches in the West, and nowhere is this plainer than in the area of the ministry. Not a few are in complete despair. Leadership fumbles. The majority carry on with little faith or hope, the idealism of their younger days buried beneath the crumbling ruins of out-moded institutions. We could liken it to a log-jam, thousands of pieces of timber jammed tightly together, suffocated and unable to move. At first sight the only remedy seems to be the use of dynamite — to blow the logs apart so that they can continue their journey down the river. Likewise there have been some radical solutions which have been suggested, which amount to something as explosive and destructive as dynamite. Is there no other way? A few years ago a woman in a Lutheran Church in San Pedro, California, pastored by Larry Christenson, had a vision of a log-jam. She was aware of the violent remedy. But then the Lord revealed to her that there was another way out, namely *to raise the level of the water,* so that the logs could be free to float away again. It is this remedy which we so badly need in our churches. The Spirit wants to make deeper channels in us, for his glory to be seen and felt. There needs to be growth in maturity before there can be growth in membership of our churches. And no amount of fiddling around in terms of re-organisation will make the slightest difference unless there is also this work of the Holy Spirit in our lives.

Now *growth* is essential for the well-being of the Church.
We have become used to this slogan in the field of economics
with its quest for the growth of the Gross National Product,
but we have become so used to stagnation in the Church that
the scandal of its failure to grow has not taken hold of us.
There is an interesting analogy in the story of the Israelites in
Egypt. The Egyptians were happy enough to have the Jews
encamp on their territory *provided they didn't grow*. The new
Pharaoh turned them into slaves for this very reason. 'He said
to the people "behold the people of Israel are too many and
too mighty for us. Come let us deal shrewdly with them, *lest
they multiply*".'[2] This has a contemporary ring about it, for it is
generally accepted that one of the main reasons for the
Catholic-Protestant conflict in Northern Ireland is the fear of
Protestants that their majority is being whittled away and the
day may soon come when the Roman Catholics outnumber
them. Pharaoh's answer to this was to make the Israelites
slaves, and keep them too busy building useless pyramids to
procreate children. And that is exactly what has happened
today, although ours is a self-inflicted wound. We have
saddled ourselves with so many organisations, tied ourselves
up with so much red-tape, stifled so much initiative, that the
Church has ceased to procreate. A falling birth-rate has
always been a sign of decadence. The Nazis gambled on their
European aggression in the 1930s because they knew that
France's birth-rate was falling.

So we see that the Israelites *had to go to grow*. They were
cramped in Egypt. They knew they had no future there. For
all subsequent generations of Jews, their release from slavery
in Egypt was to be called their 'salvation'. It is interesting to
know that a number of Hebrew words which mean "to bring
into a spacious environment", "to enlarge" and "give room
to" are used in the Old Testament to describe "salvation".[3]
So one can see how graphically this word described the
exodus from Egypt. God said he would not only set them free
from the Egyptians but also 'bring them up out of that land
to a *good and broad land*'.[4] So today the ministry needs to be

rescued from its cramped and cabined existence, and set free to develop in the power and wisdom of the Spirit. We must allow room for God to work. He needs a spacious environment to work in, not the tiny cells we offer to him.

There is another interesting aspect of this — and a further reason why the Israelites were so eager to leave Egypt. They had had enough of dictatorship. They were the victims of a centralised despotism. And so was sown in their minds the seed-thought of power sharing which was to find concrete expression in the appointing of elders.[5] From the Jewish model of plurality of leadership came ultimately the first and basic Christian pattern of leadership, as we shall see. We need to realise that Moses' desire to share his power with others had a theological as well as a pragmatic basis.[6]

If the necessity for growth is obvious, the fact that growth is not taking place is equally obvious. The early Church 'multiplied'.[7] From Pentecost onwards, we are told, 'the Lord added to their numbers day by day those who were being saved'.[8] In 1974 a report entitled *Let my people grow!* was presented to the General Synod of the Church of England.[9] It was an attempt to evaluate available statistics concerning growth in the Church of England. The report makes dismal reading. The main conclusion reached is that most churches are 'self-limiting'. That is to say the size of churches follows a simple pattern. There is some growth, but then stagnation, and, even if the population grows in the area, there is still no effective penetration of it by the Gospel. In other words spontaneous expansion is unknown. The report states: 'We have become involved in the public enactment of heresy. We believe and proclaim a Gospel of grace available to all, *but we operate a structure which takes the form of a club with limited membership.*'[10] The figures provided in the report show that churches, after initial growth, then decline before 'a steadier pattern emerges for parishes of 12,000 and over. *The growth rate slows again as population continues to rise.*'[11] The report goes on, 'The bigger the crowd the lower lay mission rate and the higher the lapse rate.' It is true that one knows of some churches that are growing in numbers, but how much of that growth is really due to people transferring their membership from another church because this particular church has a reputation for being 'alive'?

Some see the answer in terms of fewer churches and larger units. But this report shows that growth seems inevitably to lead to levelling off and stagnation. In other words our churches have not yet discovered the secret of spontaneous growth or expansion. There is an interesting parallel with economic growth. In his book *Small is Beautiful*, E. F. Schumacher shows how the expansionist economy, the principles of which were laid down by Lord Keynes, based as it is on greed and envy, carries with it the seeds of its own destruction, as we are today discovering to our cost in Western industrial society. He writes, 'After a while, even the Gross National Product refuses to rise any further, not because of scientific or technological failure, *but because of a creeping paralysis of non-cooperation.*'[12] It is being argued today by men like Dr. Schumacher and Dr. Taylor, the Bishop of Winchester, that growth is a self-destructive heresy in the field of economics. That may well be true; but it certainly is not so in church matters. The Church is in the growth business or it will die. If economic history shows that growth carries with it the seeds of its own ultimate failure, then we ought to expect churches to grow in such a way that they carry with their growth the seeds of further growth. In other words we must discover the reasons why our churches are self-limiting and discover the secrets of spontaneous expansion.

Joseph McCulloch, whom the *Sunday Times* called 'a turbulent priest', in his book *My Affair with the Church* has written about the Church as[13]

imprisoned and confused by its past, locked within outworn systems of thought and structure inhibiting that elasticity of mind and freedom of action upon which its effective ministry in the modern world entirely depends. In the existing world there is too little room for the Spirit of God to move among the dwindling number of those who still huddle within its spiritually stifling confines.

It seems as if the Church is serving a prison sentence and we need a Moses to cry 'Let my people go.' Until we emerge from the stifling confines of our prison cells, there is no hope of significant growth in our churches.

We need to remember the parables of nature. From a tiny acorn can grow an enormous oak tree. Growth is slow, but eventually it reaches saturation point. It ceases to grow any more. Nature's remedy is for the oak to go on producing more acorns which, when planted in the ground, grow into further oak trees. Thus whole forests can grow from the one original acorn. So it should be with church growth. It has to come through subdivision. The church that never plants its acorns will eventually cease to grow. This growth can only come about when we put the need for it before our personal interests, cares, likes and dislikes. Growth means discomfort and change. It means continuous adjustment to other people's needs. This can be upsetting. We become secure in our familiar groups, and find it hard to face the pain of separation. But the grain of wheat must 'fall into the ground and die' if it is to bear much fruit (John 12:24). Just as it was expedient for Jesus Christ to leave his disciples, so that they could grow and become mature, so there will be many occasions when the pain and grief of separation will be necessary for the Church to grow. Paul puts it cogently when he writes of those who will supply 'seed to the sower and bread for food' and thus 'supply and multiply your resources and increase the harvest of your righteousness' (2 Cor. 9:10). We need both bread to eat and seeds to fall into the ground if the Church is to grow.

2

The Sacred Cow of Professionalism

'Why did you call him Tortoise, if he wasn't one?' Alice asked. 'We called him Tortoise because he taught us,' said the Mock Turtle angrily, 'really you are very dull!'

Lewis Carroll, *Alice's Adventures in Wonderland*, ch. 9

WE MAY SYMPATHISE with Alice's confusion over nomenclature, but when we turn to the Christian ministry there is complete chaos. Words like "priest", "minister", "pastor" have been consistently used to describe a distinctive profession, when the New Testament uses these or similar words to describe the ministry of all the people of God. This has been pointed out many times, but the practice continues. In the same way we use the word "laity" to designate those who have not yet 'turned professional'. Since the word probably derives from the Greek word *laos*, which means "a people",[1] it is unfortunate that it has come to refer to those with amateur status. One has only to notice the tenacity with which Anglicans cling to the word "priest", to realise that it is not just a matter of words. There can lie behind our use of words a deeply entrenched attitude which can be a major hindrance to growth in the Christian Church. I refer to what the Bishop of Winchester calls in another context, the 'sacred cow of professionalism'.[2] It is not without significance that Jesus Christ only used the word "priest" once in his parables and that in a derogatory fashion. The priest in the story of the Good Samaritan was too busily religious to bother with the man bleeding in the gutter. As a young delinquent in the Bronx of New York ruefully commented, 'He knew he had been nicked.' The very confusion that reigns in the area of naming ministries is yet another symptom of the malaise that exists. If we are not clear as to the correct role that the leaders in our churches have, is it not bound to affect our churches as far as growth is concerned? What I believe we shall see is that the ministry as it is understood today not only contributes little to growth, *but can also actually hinder the church from growing*, and, alas, often does. The statistics in the workpaper, *Let my people grow!*, bear this out. Increasing the staff of a church does not lead to a significant penetration of the parish. The report tells us, 'While the present structure and lifestyle of the self-limiting congregation are retained *no amount of pastoral juggling and re-deployment of the clergy can create the needed breakthrough.*'[3] As teams of clergy increase in size a rather sinister law of diminishing returns appears to operate. But there is good reason to believe that the almost universal and traditional understanding of a professional ministry actually hinders the growth of a church.

The history of the Church in Madagascar makes interesting reading. Missionaries established the first churches on the island, but before they had time to settle down, there was a severe persecution in 1845. Missionaries were expelled and were unable to come back for twenty-five years. When eventually they were able to return they wondered if there would be any church left. To their amazement and joy they found that the church in their absence had grown tenfold. Far from being wiped out, it had prospered. It had experienced a spontaneous expansion. The missionaries set to work erecting all the paraphernalia associated with missions. Hundreds of schools were established. A theological college was founded and handsome memorial churches were erected on the sites where Christians had been martyred. *But there is no evidence that the Church continued to grow tenfold when the missionaries returned.*[4]

A few years ago I met a Pentecostal pastor from Finland who told me about a great revival in his country which led to the establishing of many more churches. I asked him how it had come about. He told me it happened in 1939. During that year war broke out between Finland and Russia. All the young men were called to the front to fight against the Russian aggressors. This included most of the Pentecostal pastors, who were comparatively young. *It was in their absence that the revival broke out.*

One of the delightful things about Juan Carlos Ortiz's controversial book *Call to Discipleship*[5] is the way he pulls the legs of ministers. He likens them to baby-sitters, for example, instead of those involved in bringing Christians to maturity.[6]

In another place he writes:[7]

> The pastor is the cork in the Church. Nobody can go out because the pastor is not perfecting the saints for the work of the ministry. Rather, he is preventing the saints from becoming ministers. It isn't that he doesn't want his people to grow; *rather, there is no room in the church structure for growth.*

This is fair comment about most churches today. In yet another passage Ortiz likens the average minister to a night-watchman guarding a pile of bricks rather than the architect instructing workers how to put the bricks together into a building.

In Charles Davis's eloquent apologia for leaving the Roman Catholic Church, written too close to unhappy events and, therefore, laced with a certain bitterness which maturer reflection might well have erased, there are some striking expressions of this clerical imprisonment the Church has built for itself.[8]

> The making of the Christian minister into a priestly class, set apart, and possessing a priesthood different in kind from the rest of Christians, disrupted the Christian community. It led to the degradation of the laity, the obscuring

of the nature of Christian life and mission, the distortion of the Christian liturgy into hieratic ritual and its eventual fossilisation... The work of Christ marked the death of all religious systems including the Jewish.... Christians had a mission to go out into the world, disclosing to men the meaning of their ordinary lives and the direction of human history as revealed in Christ. To do this they were freed from the baggage of religion, empowered by their faith and the Spirit. Instead with the creation of a special priestly class possessed of hierarchical authority, Christians have built the most elaborate religious system yet seen on earth and, imprisoned in it, are now lamenting that the course of human history has left them behind as quaint survivors of a past culture.

It is the purpose of this book to explore ways in which we can break out of the prison of our "elaborate religious system". Somehow we have to steer a careful course between anarchy, which can lead to disorderliness, and a tyranny which can impose a new form of imprisonment.

Growth does, also, have something to do with size. In the *Let my people grow!* report, it was shown that the smaller churches had proportionately better growth rates than the larger ones. Perhaps it is true, to use the Schumacher phrase, that 'small is beautiful'. There are some churches, particularly in countries where church attendance is still high, which are too large to grow properly. Like prehistoric dinosaurs, they have small heads and enormous bodies. As a result they are slow, cumbersome and clumsy, ill-adapted to change and growth. Other churches are like midgets with large heads and small bodies. It is certainly true in the economic field that a good case can be made for the small unit. Schumacher writes, 'It is moreover obvious that men organised in small units will take better care of *their* bit of land or other natural resources than anonymous companies or megalomanic governments which pretend to themselves that the whole universe is their legitimate quarry.'[9] There are churches with a large membership which makes it impossible for proper pastoral care to be exercised. But whether you subdivide the larger churches, or look for more smaller churches, the need is the same: a ministry which is adequate to cope pastorally with all the members of the church, and it is patently obvious that the ministry as it is at present structured is wholly inadequate for this task. To put it bluntly, we need a multiplication of ministers before we can hope to see a multiplication of church membership. And as things are going, that is impossible without radical re-adjustments.

Mahatma Gandhi writing about Indian economics decried a thoughtless industrialisation in which machines would 'concentrate power in a few hands and turn the masses into mere machine minders, if indeed they do not make them unemployed'. That is exactly what has happened in the Church through many centuries. Power has been concentrated in a few hands, and this has produced in the laity generations of sermon tasters and sacramentalists — watching "the machine" and taking the sacrament, rather than being actively involved in the ministry. What is even more tragic is that the end result has been like unemployment: men and women in their thousands have drifted away from the Church, bored and frustrated because of their lack of employment. Baby-sitters are all right to look after babies, but if they continue to do so when the babies have become adults, they are not going to have many customers. Ortiz tells us of an old woman he met in Argentina. He discovered she had thirty-six grandchildren. As things were going she could have 216 great-grandchildren and 1,296 great-great-grandchildren. What a high family! So Ortiz asked her how she could possibly have cared for so many.

'Oh,' she said, 'I only took care of these six. And each one of them took care of their six.'[10]

That's how the human family grows. Why should we think it is different with God's family? The finest pastor in the world cannot possibly care for 1,296 children of God! But there should be several in the congregation who can care for six.

This principle becomes clearer when we notice that, according to the New Testament, the ministry exists to facilitate growth. Chapter 4 of Paul's letter to the Ephesians is a key passage, to which we shall often turn. If we examine verses 11-16 we see that the purpose of the ministry is for the 'building up of the Body of Christ', and for 'bodily growth'. If the ministry is an inhibiting factor and slows down growth and hinders multiplication, there is something wrong with our understanding and practice of the ministry. But there is a verse in this passage, the importance of which is obscured by the intrusion of a comma. Verse 12 reads, 'His gifts were...for the equipment of the saints, for the work of ministry'. By putting a comma between these two phrases it looks as if the apostles, prophets, etc., function 'for the work of ministry'. Take away the comma and you see a new truth which bears much on the whole question of growth. The function of apostles, prophets, pastors, teachers, etc., is to equip all God's people so that they (all) can function and minister. This exegetical point is argued strongly by J. Armitage Robinson.[11] The word translated "equipment" is interesting also (*katartis-mos*). It literally means 'setting bones back into their proper place' or 'putting something back into its correct position'. If we look at it like this we may see some rays of hope for the future: in other words the role of leadership in the Church is not primarily in doing the work oneself, but in getting the whole Church to minister and so order its work that everything is in its proper and correct position. This same Greek word is used for mending fishing nets. Broken and torn nets will not catch fish, and so the fisherman has to mend them. If he doesn't, there will be no fish. So the Church will continue to fish fruitlessly if everyone is not in his correct position.

There do not lack suggestions for the correction of this serious malaise. But most of these, as we shall see, do not go deeply enough to the root of the problem. Those who have read the gloomy novels of Franz Kafka will know how they faithfully reflect the mood of his generation (he died in 1924), which saw the greatest social and political upheavals that Europe had experienced since the break-up of the Roman Empire. In Kafka's novels the individual struggles against elusive and anonymous powers. He never seems to be able to come to grips with reality. Instead, his own nightmares become reality. In *The Trial* a prison chaplain meets Joseph K. in the cathedral. Significantly he goes into the pulpit to talk to him. Joseph K. asks him to come down and sit beside him. 'I can come down now,' said the chaplain. 'I had to speak to you first from a distance. Otherwise I am too easily influenced and tend to forget my duty.'[12] So many of the modern accoutrements of religion — pulpits, dress, titles, pews and even sacraments — can be used so that they become the means of separating ministers from people and people from ministers. Ministers can speak to people at a distance, so that they can preserve sacred distinctions which God does not recognise. Pulpits can be the funk-holes of cowards too fearful to speak to their brothers face to face. Kafka's nightmare is too near reality to be comfortable for any of us. It seems that there is still a great gulf fixed between the professional ministry and ordinary people in our churches. David Sheppard, Bishop of Liverpool, has challenged the pre-suppositions of A.C.C.M., the body which selects candidates for the Anglican ministry. 'They sound to me like the expressions of a Church which reflects the hierarchies of society rather than one which challenges them. *It is determined that clergy should be professional men among other professional men.* '[13]

Perhaps the most obvious way in which the Church has tried to tackle the dead hand of professionalism has been by releasing the so-called frozen assets of the Church — the laity. This has been the policy of all churches in recent years. Sometimes this has come about through theological conviction, sometimes because of sheer expediency. The matter figured prominently in the Vatican II discussions on the nature of the Church. Archbishop Stourm, for example, said:[14]

There do not exist two churches: one which teaches and acts, the other passive, which permits itself to be taught, doing nothing else... Because they have their proper and irreplaceable role in the Church, the laity demand to be treated as adults...to be given real responsibilities, to participate in its life and action.[14]

But the point seems to have escaped so many advocates of the mobilising of the laity that *ministers also need to be released*. If the cork is still firmly in the bottle, the only way the laity can free themselves is by bursting the bottle. And that is what some are choosing to do because they cannot abide any longer the heavy hand of authority or the insipid leadership which some are giving. We cannot blame the laity if they move out of Egypt and leave the ministers behind, if the ministers are doing nothing about it.

Another attempt to set the Church free can be seen in the democratisation of our churches. This expresses itself in the desire to let everyone have a say in church government. And so we have had the move, for example, in the Church of England, towards synodical government. But the old barriers often remain. The caste system is much the same. And no system of government can change inherited prejudices. Synodical government, with its division into "houses", is still perpetuating the concept of the ministry as 'special, dignified and different', as the Bishop of Liverpool has described it.

There are other remedies which have been suggested. For some the answer lies in the redeployment of ministers. Others are pressing for changing the titles of ministers and dropping the terms 'Revd', 'Most Revd', 'Venerable', etc. Others are avoiding clerical dress such as clerical collars and cassocks. Others see the hope for the future in the ordination of women. Yet others are pressing for more authority in the Church. But all these familiar antidotes, which may be good in themselves, are simply pruning the branches. We must get at the root if we are to see a deep and lasting change.

There is another approach which some are making. They

see the hope of the future in the charismatic renewal. The change will come, so charismatic people argue, when ministers and lay people are filled with the Holy Spirit. But the charismatic renewal has been going long enough now for all to see that it isn't a panacea for all the ills in the Church. It does not guarantee growth. Its emphasis on the need for the power of the Spirit is important. Its new insights into the use of charismatic gifts, and of "every-member ministry" should be the norm in all churches. But experience has shown that where there is a receiving of new wine without a complementary new wineskin, the renewal peters out, for it hasn't really got to the roots of our spiritual malaise. It can even be a distraction from the real renewal that God wants to bring. In the Church of the Redeemer, Houston, the revolution which took place was more than a receiving of power; it was when the church became open to a new-look kind of ministry as well as a new way of living, and was free to develop new structures to contain the new wine of the Spirit, that it developed as fully as it did. Ministers who have been martinets *before* their experience of the Spirit do not always change afterwards. Of course, altering the system itself is no answer either. We do need the new wine of the Spirit. But if the new wine is not in new wineskins flexible enough to contain it, it will simply burst the skins, and the wine will be lost. When people begin to grow strongly in the Spirit they need room to manoeuvre. If we want to see church growth (and who doesn't?), we must allow room for it.

All these suggestions can help. The laity do need to be released still further. Some ministers do need to be redeployed. Our nomenclature for the ministry is confused and inaccurate. Democracy, properly understood, is good. We all need to be filled with the Spirit. But none of those really deals with the crux of the problem, a professionalism which claims far too much power and attention. To ordain women will only add to the confusion; it will simply perpetuate the caste system, only include women as well as men. We shall be no better off.

But there are signs of hope. If most of these are to be seen in the world rather than in the Church it need not daunt us. First of all, we have seen in the last few decades several liberating movements. This century has seen, for example, the fuller emancipation of women, so that they are able to share equally with men in the rights and responsibilities of citizenship. Whatever the rights or wrongs of the ordination of women, men and women sharing in the ministry no longer provide the scandal of previous centuries. Again, universal education and the spectacular rise in literacy mean that the average layman is often as well educated as the minister, and sometimes better. There has also been a subtle but significant movement away from the strict hierarchical structuring of society. This is a process that has been going on since the collapse of the feudal system, but it has greatly accelerated through the influence of egalitarian revolutions and the rise and influence of the United States and Russia as countries which in their different ways have sought to do away with class distinction.

There are two other factors which bear on the ministry. One of these is the gradual elimination of *distance,* which has in the past been a barrier to communication. Alongside the growth of huge international businesses, which are able to function and be co-ordinated because of technology such as Telex systems and speedy jet travel for their executives, the world-wide Church, if not always adventurous enough to use modern technology, is in a much better position to be co-ordinated and to experience healthy cross-fertilisation of ideas and ministries.

A further factor is the sense of immediacy which dominates the thinking of modern people. Ours is an age which thinks in functional terms. The whole concept of "indelibility" which has dominated the Church's concept of the ministry for centuries is anathema to the modern mind. The Bishop of Winchester has written: [15]

An *ad hoc* response is the only kind of obedience which

rings true to many of the liveliest young Christians today. They will give themselves to meet a need without reserve, but also without pretensions. They will serve without a label. A call makes sense to them but not a vocation.. The only response they can make with integrity is 'I will go now... How can I tell what the opening will be after that?'

Thus many people may respond to a temporary or part-time call to ministry who would not be prepared to commit themselves to a full-time life-long vocation. A Roman Catholic writes in the same vein: 'It seems to me that we may have to return to the sense of the priest's role as much less permanent and much more intermittent.'[16]

Even if in some ways what is happening in the world seems to be bypassing the Church, which often seems to have an infallible built-in resistance to any change, there are other things which are taking place which are forcing the Church to change, whether it likes it or not. World inflation, for example, has dealt a body blow to the Church, from which its finances may never recover. Churches are unable to maintain the old structures any more, and worse is probably yet to come. It is not beyond the bounds of possibility that ministers may have to face redundancy. Already the Episcopal Church of Scotland, which unlike the Church of England has few endowments, has had to face this question, for it no longer has the financial resources to support a full-time professional ministry to the extent it has in the past. If necessity is the mother of invention, there is hope that a financial crisis in the Church will force it to change its inbred attitudes with regard to ministry.

Of course the Church is not to ape the world. The Church ought to be both an example to the world and a catalyst to provide changes in society. It has been both of these things at times in the past. But it seems to have lost its nerve. It is not short of good ideas, but it has a fatal inability to put into action what it sees to be right. One cannot but conclude that the desire to defend clerical professionalism and the fear of losing status stymie every bold plan for change. Terry Eagleton in the Roman Catholic magazine *New Blackfriars* makes a radical appraisal of this:[16]

Why this [the priest's role] involves wearing a black suit and being celibate and spending his time between liturgical activities in generally fostering Christian welfare seems to me much less obvious. I don't think we will ever have a really non-paternalist church until priests (and I think the word 'priest' has to go, as well as the word 'minister' which again suggests a kind of specific relationship) are ordinary workers with families who have this special function to celebrate the liturgy within a church where the activities of teaching, welfare and preaching are genuinely common, and not the monopoly of a caste.

The Church has certainly not lacked those who have pointed to this radical change of emphasis and outlook. But something more is necessary.

We must let a layman have the final word. George Goyder expresses the frustrations of a layman in his book *The People's Church*, with the sub-title *A Layman's Plea for Partnership*. He writes:[17]

Why is it that the Church today will not trust its members? Why does the Church so often decline to recognise and to accept the activity of the Spirit among unregulated groups of Christians? Why is all initiative in the Church expected and presumed to derive from the clergy? *It is because we have substituted for the biblical doctrine of the Holy Spirit as ruler in the Church, a doctrine of our own, unknown to scripture, the authority of professionalism.* (Italics mine).

Introduction
Clearer Thinking

Double think means the power of holding two contradictory beliefs in one's mind simultaneously and accepting both of them.

George Orwell *1984*

WE LIVE IN a world where there is much double thinking, and George Orwell's picture of the future is becoming more and more true. Politicians, lawyers, scientists and economists have proved their prowess at holding and accepting diametrically opposite viewpoints at the same time.

The story of Peter walking on the water is familiar to us. In Matt. 14:31 Jesus said to Peter, 'O man of little faith, why did you doubt?' The Greek word for doubt (*distazo*) is an interesting one. The commonly held view of this story is that Peter looked away from Jesus and saw the waves. But the use of this verb suggests something different. The word literally means 'standing and looking where two ways come together'. The truth is that Peter looked first at Jesus, then at *Jesus and the waves simultaneously*. Dick Mills, commenting on this interpretation, writes, 'Peter was pulled apart by double vision. He was seeing two opposites at the same time with the same gaze.' If you are taking a photograph of a distant mountain you focus your camera on infinity. If you are doing a close-up of a person, you set your camera focus on the distance between the camera and the person. You have to make up your mind which you want to photograph. If you want to focus on both at the same time, and split the difference, both the mountain and the person will be out of focus.

In this book we have to do some careful and accurate focusing. We have already seen how blurred the whole subject is. If we try to focus it all at the same time we shall sink like Peter! So we shall stick very closely to an important order, and be careful, too, about our terminology.

We are covering a subject which has been much discussed and debated. There are large areas of disagreement amongst Christians. Many books have been written. So we shall be trying all the time to focus on essential principles, the irreducible minimum necessary if the Church is to minister effectively.

We need also to rediscover the principle of flexibility which was so clearly visible in the early Church. It is not a new system we need, but a new open-ness to hear the Holy Spirit directing us. He will not tell us all to do the same thing. Ministry in the New Testament developed within a Church which had not erected cumbersome structures, but was remarkably resilient in the face of change around it. There were no stereotypes. They had no blueprints, and neither should we have any, for this is the way to kill the spontaneity which the early Christians so obviously possessed. We should hesitate before being dogmatic about "office", when the New Testament is very much more concerned about "function".

We have also to be careful about our attitude to the past. In one of his earliest speeches as Prime Minister, Sir Winston Churchill said, 'If the present tries to sit in judgment on the past, it will lose the future.' We must certainly learn from the past, both its successes and failures, but it is not for us to condemn those in the past who did not see what we now see. Neither should we regard radical changes as disloyalty to them. We have to answer to God — not to men.

Order of Subjects

The book is basically divided into three parts:

Part I

Deals with what *ministry* is and the different spheres of ministry. We also look at the divine pattern seen in the ministry of the Son and of the Holy Spirit. We recognise the New Testament emphasis on *service,* and examine the charismatic dimension of ministry.

Part II

Recognises that ministry is for the Body of Christ, and so we need to distinguish between the local church and the catholic or universal Church. We shall look into the contemporary discussion on the ministry of women in the Church, and the place of discipline, authority and commitment. We shall also consider the question whether the New Testament is a blue-print or not *before* actually going on to deal with the matter of Christian leadership.

Part III

Is concerned with leadership in the local and universal Church; who these leaders should be and how they should be trained and set apart or ordained for their ministry.

The order is important. We need to recapture the *scope* of Christian ministry before we can consider its application to the Church itself. Leadership is not the sum of all Christian ministry but one aspect of that ministry, and that is why we have left it to last.

Basic propositions

Before we plunge into the book we need to grasp four basic propositions. These may be controverted by some, but for the purpose of clarity we shall stick consistently to them throughout the book. Where the matter is controversial, there will be reasoned arguments for the stance one takes.

Proposition No. 1

The word 'ministry' applies to all members of the Body of Christ, not to a select coterie. This book then is for all those who are concerned to serve Christ and his people.

Proposition No. 2

In terms of ministry there is no distinction in the New Covenant between male and female, and so the word 'man' embraces woman too. This is an assumption that obviously needs defending, and this will be done in chapter 8.

Proposition No. 3

Although all members of Christ's Body are called to *minister,* not all are called to *lead.* Leadership is a ministry in the Body of Christ, and when we come to consider it, our main concern is with the concept of leadership in the Church rather than with what various churches have called their leaders. The words which are in current use are often confusing, and tend to perpetuate confused thinking about ministry. So we are sticking to the simple and common expression *leaders,* although when we deal with supra-local leadership, we shall use the term "bishop" because of its traditional use from the second century to the present time.

Proposition No. 4

We propose to consider the Church in two senses. First, in the sense of the Catholic or universal Church, and secondly in that of the local church. We shall distinguish between them simply by using a capital C when we are referring to the universal Church, and a small c when we refer to the local church. We shall explain the reasons for this in chapter 7. When we refer to a denomination, such as the Methodist Church, we shall use the capital C.

It is important that we bear these propositions in mind, even if we disagree with them at this stage, for it is easy to confuse issues by a loose use of words like 'Church', 'ministry', and 'ministers'. If we are to focus clearly on the biblical principles of Christian growth, we need to keep these propositions before us as we examine this subject.

Finally we need to look at the word "priest". For some it will be a surprise to find in this book little or nothing about priesthood. It is well known that the word is used in the New Testament to describe a function of all God's people, the 'priesthood of all believers', never in the limited sense it is used today. To some the word "priest" is meaningful, but it is difficult to see how the principles outlined in this book can be established if we persist in using the word in this restricted sense. Archbishop Cranmer understood the word "priest" to have derived from the word "presbyter". But many see the function of a priest, especially at the altar and in the confessional, quite differently from that of a presbyter. One fears that the widespread and erroneous use of the word "priest" has been a cause of spiritual decline, for it has shifted the emphasis of the ministry from the personal to the liturgical, increased clerical professionalism, and inhibited the development of the charism of leadership. We need to drop the word "priest" from our vocabulary and restore the ministry of the presbyterate to its rightful and scriptural position.

Part I

The Church and its Ministry

3

What it is all About

And Christ's gifts were that some should be apostles, some prophets, some evangelists, some pastors and teachers, for the equipment of the saints, for the work of ministry, for building up the body of Christ. Eph. 4:11-12.

So FAR WE have established that the Church is meant to grow, both in maturity and in membership, and that the ministry of the Church is meant to help it to grow. But in practice the Church is not growing in most of the Western world, and the ministry itself can be more of a hindrance than a help. There are few signs of significant change in this depressing picture. There are a few churches which are growing, but often a large factor in such growth is the transfer of members from weaker churches rather than addition from the area of the un-churched masses, and this is particularly true in industrial and the more densely populated urban areas.

David Edwards, in his book *Religion and Change,* writes, 'It is clear that the domineering clericalism which has afflicted almost all the churches has been a betrayal of the very idea of the Christian minister, and it is not surprising that a revolt has resulted.' [1] We have tended to play down what has in fact been disastrous. It is difficult to draw conclusions from the statistics, for we have no way of discovering the numbers of men who might otherwise have been trained and ordained to full-time ministry. But the numbers are probably high. In a passage about the future leadership of the Church, David Edwards writes,

'The Church which wrote the New Testament felt the power of its living Lord in its own life — and if Christianity is not to be reduced to rootless, shapeless democracy, the Lordship of Christ over the Church must be recovered for our time. Many are coming to the conclusion that one way of bearing witness to this Lordship is to recover the leadership of the ministers of the Church — *but it must be a leadership with a difference.*' (Italics mine)

Before we can begin to consider what Christian leadership is all about — leadership with a difference — we need to look closely at what 'ministry' itself is. The New Testament is very much more interested in ministry than in "ministers" as such, for all God's people are called to be ministers, whereas not all are called to be leaders. We also need to see the importance of ministry in growth situations, for its proper understanding and ordering is crucial when the Church begins to grow. Without correct structuring, as we have painfully discovered, the growth rate slows down and there comes stagnation and even loss. Growth is not the answer to every problem, but rather it creates a whole new set of problems, as the early Christians soon found out. In those early days it was the needs of the hour which determined the nature of the ministry more than any other factor. Later generations have tended to read back into the New Testament principles which the early Christians themselves were probably totally unaware of.

The popular image of ministry today is dominated by religious ritual. Ministers take services, preach sermons, raise money, baptise people, marry couples and bury the dead. But one really hopeful sign today is the switch of emphasis from office to function. Thus Hans Küng writes, 'Ecclesial office is not a New Testament notion, but a problematical concept which emerged from later reflections.'[2] He goes on to show that the New Testament emphasis was on *service* rather than status. He writes, 'Of course there is authority in the Church, but there is no legitimate authority other than that established upon service and not in force, prerogatives and privileges, which would *require* service. Were one to formulate the matter more precisely in theological terms, it would be preferable to speak of ecclesial *service* rather than of ecclesial "office".'[3]

The spotlight in our day is more and more being put on Ephesians 4 as a definitive chapter on ministry in the Bible. After writing about the essential unity of the Church and the ascension of Christ to his heavenly position, Paul talks about the gifts of Christ to the Church. (The word *dōrea*, not *charismata*, is used by the apostle in v. 7). 'Some should be apostles, some prophets, some evangelists, some pastors and teachers...for building up the body of Christ.'[4] This passage figures prominently in the whole contemporary debate on the Christian ministry. Ephesians is one of the later writings in the New Testament. This is not the place to examine the controversy amongst scholars over its authorship. The important thing to notice is that the author is concerned about a wider context than the local church. He has a more catholic concern for the health and growth of the whole Christian Church. David Sheppard (Bishop of Liverpool) refers in this passage to 'the five callings',[5] and regards them as 'highly relevant' to ministry in urban and industrial areas. The charismatic renewal has also majored on this passage, and Juan Carlos Ortiz in his book *Call to Discipleship* makes much of it.[6]

I believe that it is much more helpful to see these five callings as five spheres of ministry rather than five "offices" to which men are appointed or ordained. This is not to say there may not be a person who is fairly obviously a pastor or another a teacher. However, the New Testament is far more concerned with function than office, and in any case there are problems as to whether we should be looking for apostles and prophets today, and we shall be dealing with this matter in chapter 12. Also the terms "pastor" and "teacher" do not seem to have been applied even in the New Testament to definite offices, and the word "evangelist" is only used once in the New Testament of a person (Philip in Acts 21:8). Paul uses it to describe part of the ministry of Timothy (2 Tim. 4:5). But he could equally have applied it to any other leader in the early Church, and there is no indication that Timothy was a specialist "evangelist" in the sense that we use the term today. The word does not come in any other of Paul's lists of ministries (e.g. 1 Cor. 12:28). It is better to see these five ministries as five spheres, rather like the Olympic symbol, all inter-related to each other. People may well have an ability or *charisma* to function effectively in several areas of these ministries. One knows, for example, of some people who are gifted both as teachers *and* pastors. Similarly one knows of some good teachers who have slender pastoral abilities, and pastors who are not effective at communicating truth. All one can say is that the universal Church in general and the local church in particular needs a combination of all these "callings" or "spheres of ministry", and that they should especially be seen in Christian leadership. This leads one to see the importance of team ministries and collegial leadership, both in the local church and trans-locally, in which the leaders are gifted in each of these areas, so that the whole team has all of these gifts, and in that sense are Christ's gift to the Church for its blessing and growth. Like the different vitamins, all of which are necessary for the healthiness of the physical body, all of these are necessary for the healthy growth of the Body of Christ. We can think of them as five slogans:

Let my people go — the apostolic function of the Church
Let my people hear — the prophetic function of the Church
Let my people care — the pastoral function of the Church
Let my people know — the teaching function of the Church

Let my people grow — the evangelistic function of the Church

Or as five commands of the Lord:

Go to my people — Speak to my people — Care for my people — Teach my people — Reach my people.

We must then label all five spheres of ministry "for service". The service of God and his people should be the overriding motive and incentive for all ministry. That was the reason Moses gave to Pharaoh why God's people were to be released from their captivity. 'Let my people go that they may serve me' (Exod. 9:1). The basic reason for all ministry should be *service*.

It is also important to see the relationship that all these spheres of ministry have to God's Word. Some of the original apostles were those entrusted with passing on the actual words of our Lord, later to become the canon of the New Testament.

Prophets are those who hear God speaking and pass on what they hear to others. Pastors are primarily concerned with "feeding" the flock God has entrusted to them,[7] and both teachers and evangelists would see their chief role in these terms. When we come to consider "offices" we shall again see how important God's Word is in relationship to leadership in the Church. In the list of gifts for charismatic ministry in 1 Cor. 12:8-10, the majority of them are concerned with speaking words to people or to God.

We need to look more closely and practically as to what we mean by each of these spheres of ministry. But before we do that we should consider another aspect of ministry in general which is fundamental to our understanding of it. For centuries man's understanding of God has tended to begin at the point of the incarnation and redemption of Christ, meeting man at the point of his sin and its need for forgiveness, rather than at the doctrine of creation, meeting man at the point of his humanity. Thus many writers on the subject of the Christian ministry begin with the pattern of

Christ's ministry. For example, the 1973 Anglican-Roman Catholic Statement on Ministry and Ordination says, 'The life and self-offering of Christ perfectly expresses what it is to serve God and man. *All Christian ministry...flows and takes its shape from this* source and model.' (Italics mine).[8] But the ministry of Christ began at creation, and we must not forget the many hidden yet creative years spent at the carpenter's bench in Nazareth. Man's ministry also began in the Garden of Eden before man's fall and eviction from paradise. Arnold Bittlinger, in his book *Gifts and Ministries,*[9] rightly begins his study of stewardship in Genesis, and draws our attention to the stewardship entrusted by God to man and woman: 'Be fruitful and multiply, and fill the earth and subdue it; and have dominion over the fish of the sea and over the birds of the air and over every living thing that moves upon the earth.'[10] In the next chapter God is depicted as a gardener who entrusts his garden to man to 'till it and keep it'. The first "ministry" that God entrusted to man was to do with the earth, not the Spirit. God created the world, and then delegated authority over it and responsibility to care for it to man. But since God had created man in his own image, he entrusted his creation to those in whom was a spirit of creativity. In other words this was God's "Yes" to science, technology, poetry, music — and all that we tend to classify as culture and civilisation. Man has not always been worthy of God's trust, and the effect of the Fall has at times warped man's understanding of his stewardship in God's world.

This has come to the fore in recent years and been expressed anxiously by a growing number of conservationists. Thus John Taylor refers in his book *Enough is Enough* to the 'global gardyloo', the problems of modern effluence which have turned many of the rivers and lakes of the world into massive unflushed lavatories.[11] Mercury poisoning off the southern shores of Japan; the death of forty million fish in the Rhine in 1969; hepatitis contracted on the beaches near Rome, and the death of many of the Swiss and Italian lakes, former beauty-spots, all point to man's untrustworthiness in the world of which he is supposed to be God's steward. When we remember the wholesale slaughter of animals and the elimination of hundreds of species by the indiscriminate use of insecticides and by man's lust for killing, we see how far man has fallen from his ideals. For example, in only thirty years the total blue whale population of the world has dropped from 100,000 to 1,000 or less.[12] God's steward soon became a rebel who interpreted his stewardship in terms of irresponsible hedonism. Ecologists now say there is a limit to this, beyond which man will destroy himself as well.

It is vital that in seeing ministry in the Church we do not forget the creative ministry which God has also entrusted to man. When we come to the controversial issue of the ministry of women, it is important for us to see the significance of the original partnership God created between man and woman, which, though impaired like everything else by the Fall, is still part of God's plan for ministry today. We need to see that, whatever else ministry may be, it is intended to be part of God's re-creative activity and his plans for the transformation of his creation. In other words, *all ministry should be creative.* This is one of the reasons why we should avoid the stereotype like the plague. The pooling of the gifts of a body of people who present great variety in terms of age, income, background, culture, race and education, is the work of master craftsmen. It is the creation by God's grace of a single work of art. When ministry fails, there is division, a spirit of competitiveness, pride and prejudice, jealousy and private interests — all too common, alas, in our churches. But when the Spirit is in command and the ministry is functioning properly, then a bunch of individuals is set free from their individualism, united into a body, and liberated to function as individuals in a team of people. That calls for creative leadership, and when it happens God's creative work is again bearing fruit in the world.

But it isn't just in personal relationships that ministry should be creative. It ought also to express itself physically and literally in the things that people do when they come together. It should be expressed in the music they write, the songs they sing, the liturgy they enact, the buildings they design, the prayers they pray, the *charismata* they manifest, and so on. The Holy Spirit was involved in creating things long before he became involved in church growth and development. The failure of the Church to express adequately the creative instincts implanted in man by God can be seen in formal liturgy, ugly buildings, slushy songs, pious prayers, disorderly meetings and general lack of imagination or even concern, as well as in poor human relationships and a harmful individualism on the one hand and a dull uniformity or herd instinct on the other.

It is not without significance that the profession chosen by the Son of God should have been carpentry, for in it he combined both creative and redemptive work. He would have been involved in both making and re-making or repairing wooden things. He grew up concerned with shape and order; with symmetry and design; with the creation of beauty without the loss of utility; with variety yet unity; with repairing broken and worn out objects. In our wasteful society the art of repairing broken things has been all but lost, for they are simply discarded. I knew once of a man who made a point of collecting pots, pans and kettles in the bazaars of India which had been repaired, sometimes so many times that they bore little resemblance to the original. There was a new kind of beauty in these extraordinary items of hardware. So the Son of God delights in repairing broken people. He rejects no one, and so the Spirit of Christ releases in us that gift of creativity, so that ministry in the Church can be seen as the divine craft of knitting together people into creative relationships with one another. In no way is it to be seen in terms of crushing or manipulating people. Rather is it to be seen in releasing personal potential so that each can contribute to the other, and the whole present itself as a glorious mosaic of many pieces in a true unity. Such is the art and craft of Christian ministry, in which leadership plays an important part. And God is not interested in stereotypes.

There should be infinite variety in the spheres of Christian ministry. We should now look carefully at each of these areas.

The apostolic role of the Church

This is of supreme importance. Paul places apostles at the head of his lists of ministries. In this chapter, as we have already pointed out, we are concerned with apostolic function rather than apostles as such. The word *apostolos* means first of all "messenger" or "emissary", and it was often used in Hellenistic Greek in the context of the sea. It was sometimes used to describe, for example, a fleet or an expedition of ships. Sometimes it was used to describe the admiral who commanded the ships. But it also has a Jewish background. In later Judaism the "apostles" were ordained rabbis who travelled to the Jews of the *diaspora*. As Arnold Bittlinger points out, Saul of Tarsus was probably ironically called an apostle when he went to Damascus to arrest Christians![12] There was an old Jewish maxim, 'The apostle is the equivalent of him who has sent him.' So in Matthew 10:40 we find Jesus saying, 'He who receives you receives me', and in Luke 10:16, 'He who hears you hears me.'

The point which is common to both the Jewish and the Greek concepts of apostleship is that apostles are those who travel as representatives. The word "representative" is sometimes used today as a synonym for a travelling salesman. The apostle is one who is sent on a mission or expedition, and in obedience *goes*. We can say, then, that the apostolic role of the Church is concerned with "going" or "moving", and those involved in this ministry will be often on the move.

As we look at each of these spheres of ministry, we shall find that the ministry of God, the Father, the Son, and the Holy Spirit is the prototype and inspiration of all apostolic ministry. God calls his people to be a "pilgrim people" because He is a pilgrim God, who is always "on the move" — actively engaged in the welfare and well-being of his people. And it is no accident that Abraham, the founder of the Jewish race, should have been called to leave his country and relatives and go to an unknown destination. Dr. J. Fison, the late Bishop of Salisbury, once wrote [13]

> the story of Acts is the story of the stupendous missionary achievement of a community inspired to make a continual series of creative experiments by the pentecostal Spirit. Against a static church, unwilling to obey the guidance of the Spirit, no gates of any sort are needed to oppose its movement, *for it does not move.* But against a Church that is on the move, inspired by the pentecostal Spirit, neither the 'gates of hell' nor any other gates can prevail.

So both the pioneer patriarch in the Old Testament and the pioneer apostles in the New expressed their commitment and call in terms of movement. It is one of the tragic facts of Church history that, because the Church itself has settled so often for the soft option of "staying put", the Holy Spirit has stirred up movements, which are God's second best, and which have to live dangerously close all the time to schism. That schism takes place at many times is as much due to the stubborn refusal on the part of the established Church to see facts as it is to the immature impatience of enthusiasts. The Church seems so often to have an inherent conservatism which prevents it from taking its opportunities when the Spirit presents them. The history of the charismatic movement so far has run pretty true to type. Some Christian leaders have been slow to come to terms with it, or even to begin to understand it or know how to harness its potential for the good of the entire Church. They are mostly content that it does no great harm. They act as referees rather than as team captains involved in the action. They only make their presence felt when there is a foul, especially when the crowd has seen it, so that failure to do anything may cause a riot or serious breach of the peace. Christian leaders are supposed to lead. An apostolic church demands firm leadership. A church which does not move can get by without it. But a moving and a growing church must have apostolic leadership.

Apostolic ministry always comes into its own in periods of Christian revival and renewal. We have only to think of Francis of Assisi and his roving monks; or of Theresa of Avila, who was once called by the Papal Nuncio 'that restless, disobedient, contumacious gadabout'; or of George White-field and John Wesley; or of the less well known William Grimshaw, who spent only the weekends in his Yorkshire parish of Haworth, and the rest of the week preaching and teaching up and down the Yorkshire dales, to the chagrin of his neighbouring clergy but the secret delight of his bishop! Whether it is Gladys Aylward in China, Cable and French in Mongolia, Francis Xavier in India, or the men who brought the Gospel to Britain and the continent of Europe — the Kilians, Columbas, Patricks, Aidans and a thousand and one others — the Church at its best has been thoroughly apostolic. When the Church becomes sleepy and self-indulgent, when 'establishment' is the vogue, then God sends forth apostolic ministries.

The prophetic role of the Church

If apostolic ministry is in short supply in times of spiritual decline, so are prophets. There can be plenty of false prophets, as the true prophets in the Old Testament are quick to point out, who prophesy out of their own heads, but there are times when the word of the Lord is "rare" and there is "no frequent vision".[14] There may be teachers and pastors. But the Church and the world miss something vital when the voice of the true prophet is no longer heard in the land.

We are living in days which are not exactly calculated to encourage the career of a prophet. If the main function of an apostle is to "go", then the main function of a prophet is to "listen". The Church today is notoriously bad at listening and being still and quiet enough to do so. It talks and writes incessantly, but where are the people who know how to retreat from the world and listen to God?

We have bred a whole new race who have never learnt the art of listening to the Lord, and passing on his word to others.

A prophet is not a scripture exegete. He knows the scriptures, but he does not teach from his knowledge of the Bible, which is the role of the teacher; he hears that which is particularly appropriate for the hour, and he faithfully passes on the message to the appropriate quarter, wherever and whoever that may be.

We are not here concerned about the office of a prophet, and whether we are justified today in looking for those who are called by God to fulfil such an appointment. Our concern is with the *function* of prophecy. Michael Green in his book, *Evangelism in the Early Church*, describes how such people were used in the first three centuries of the Christian Church.[15]

> Prophecy was coherent speech, under the direct domination of the Holy Spirit. It was exercised by men and women alike and appears to have been very varied in content... This direct word from God must, if it be genuine, be in accord with the content of the apostolic faith.

It seems to have been a form of preaching, too, and was much used in the early church in evangelism. Prophecy declined as episcopacy grew in influence, but according to Michael Green, 'it continued well into the third century and made a great impression on ordinary people'.

The prophets in both the Old and New Testaments were people who had spiritual insight, which they received from God, largely as a result of prayer and waiting upon him, and leading a life of separation from the world as far as possible. The divine aspect is all important, for in our day we have tended to shift the emphasis. A Christian prophet today is often seen as a person who has a full grasp and understanding of the world — and courage and wisdom to pronounce on it. Prophecy has three main aspects. The first is the simple and straightforward 'forth-telling', or speaking the words that God has given. An example of this was God's answer to Moses' plea, 'I am not eloquent'. God appointed Aaron as his mouthpiece. 'He shall speak for you to the people; and he shall be a mouth for you, and you shall be to him as God.'[16] Aaron was in effect Moses' prophet. In a similar manner the prophet stands in relationship to God himself. But the prophets also *foretold* the future. As time went on this became increasingly their role in the Old Testament, and in the New Testament we find prophets doing the same thing (e.g. Agabus, Acts 11:28; 21:10). Thus Jeremiah was unpopular when he foretold the capture of Jerusalem. But there is also a third element in prophecy. It is a kind of eighth sense, an ability to see what is invisible, hear what is inaudible, and touch what is intangible. Elisha, for example, had the reputation of knowing what was said in secret many miles away (2 Kings 6:12), and Ezekiel, though resident in Babylon, had an uncanny knowledge of Jerusalem (Ezek. chs 8, 9). Peter had the same gift when he saw through the subterfuge of Ananias and Sapphira (Acts 5).

We see all three elements of prophecy in the ministry of Christ, particularly in the story of his conversation with the woman at the well-side in John 4. Jesus spoke forth to her the word of God — 'If you knew the gift of God, and who it is that is saying to you, "give me a drink", you would have asked him and he would have given you living water' (v. 10). He later on foretold the future. 'The hour is coming, when neither on this mountain nor in Jerusalem will you worship the Father' (v. 21). And when He said to the woman, 'Go call your husband', she replied, 'I have no husband', and he said to her, 'You have had five husbands, and he whom you now have is not your husband' (v. 18). So Jesus revealed his ability to see right into people and know the hidden facts. No wonder this woman cried out in astonishment, 'Sir, I perceive that you are a prophet' (v. 19).

How desperately the Church today needs people who are prophets in these three ways: able to speak clearly and practically God's word for the hour; able to foretell the future and so warn the Church of dangers and changes so that it can steer a safe course; able to discern the secrets of men's hearts and so deliver discussion and counselling from unreality. But prophets are not popular people to have around. To yearn for the Church again to put on the prophet's mantle will lead it to much disturbance and even anger. When my wife and I were in Pakistan in 1975 we had a session with the Bishop of Karachi, and he told us this interesting story. Some months before we arrived, an African called to see the bishop. He claimed to have been sent by his church in Nigeria to minister in the diocese of Karachi. When the Bishop asked him who he was he told him, 'I am a prophet.' He actually produced his passport to prove it, and sure enough written after the word "occupation" was the single word "prophet"! And there he stood in the Bishop's office, without any money, but claiming to have been sent by his church in Nigeria. A few days later his credentials arrived from Africa. He belonged to a *bona fide* church, so the Bishop let him loose in the diocese. When I asked the Bishop what happened he told me, 'That man did more good in our diocese in six months than anyone else who has come.' When I asked what he had done, the Bishop replied, 'He just sorted people out.' Apparently he had not been very popular, but had broken through certain forms of superficiality, and brought a very welcome stream of reality. He was really a prophet, and the diocese benefited enormously. Our mind very naturally turns to the New Testament prophets who similarly travelled around "sorting people out". It is often a helpful thing to have some outsider who has no particular axe to grind, but who has prophetic insights, to come into a difficult situation and bring the hidden things to light.

But the local church needs this prophetic instinct. It needs leaders and people who know how to receive a message from God and who are faithful and courageous at bringing it to the right quarters in the right spirit. At every level of church life it is vital that God should be able to say and do what he wants to. And if we move into the wider field of the universal Church, we need men who can speak to the world about its problems and needs, not with worldly wisdom, but with a heavenly wisdom, bringing God's verdict and view to bear upon concrete situations, as the Old Testament prophets did in their day.

The pastoral role of the Church

The Church should not only be a body that moves with God and hears his word; it should also be a *caring* community. The psalmist in Psalm 23 declares that God is his shepherd. In Ezekiel 34 the prophet thunders against the shepherds of Israel who have been 'feeding themselves' rather than feeding the sheep. The sheep have been shamelessly exploited. The weak have not been strengthened, the sick have not been healed, the crippled have not been bound up, the strayed have not been brought back, the lost have not been sought, and they have been ruled over 'with force and harshness'. Here is a tragic picture of sheep being "scattered" because they have no shepherds, and becoming "food for all the wild beasts". God declares himself "against the shepherds" and promises to 'rescue my sheep from their mouths'. And then God himself undertakes to be shepherd to them.

Unfortunately this is all too accurate a description of much of the Church today. Without proper pastoral care the Church will not grow, and it is hopelessly impractical to expect one man, or even a team of ministers, to cope with the pastoral needs of an entire church. The larger the church, and the more it grows, the more difficult it is to provide proper pastoral care for the members. It is one area of ministry that has to be organised, or it will never be done properly. A haphazard approach is bound to be inadequate. A shepherd needs to know his sheep and call them by name. If the sheep are multiplying, then the shepherds must multiply also. Therein often lies the principal fault in church organisation. Because of the basic one-man or professional style of ministry, it is impossible to cope properly with growth, and so it falls off. Here is the nub of our problem.

But, first, we need to see what pastoral care involves. It involves knowing the "sheep". It includes looking after them, caring for each part of their lives, and helping them to grow in Christ and to relate well with other people. It involves their physical and psychological well-being; this will include the ministry of healing. It includes their practical day-to-day lives, seeing that their marriages are healthy, that they have got the right attitude to their work, and know how to look after their financial affairs. It may include help and advice in bringing up their children. It will include teaching about every aspect of life, including stewardship of money and time, discipline of life, how to overcome temptation, and how to know the guidance of God. It entails seeing that their knowledge of God and his word is increasing and they are being obedient to it. Such pastoral concern is impossible for one man or a team of ministers. The only answer is to train shepherds, who are themselves being shepherded by others, so that a pastoral network of care and concern is built up in the church, with everyone taken care of. In the early Church this was the instinctive desire of those who had been called to be shepherds, namely, the apostles. But when they found it impossible to deal adequately with everyone, and realised that they were neglecting their particular apostolic role, they had men appointed who could deal with the practical pastoral needs of the Greek widows (Acts 6). They recognised that it was something that needed to be done. There was no question about that. But the answer was *not* to stop the growth pattern of the Church, but to delegate the ministry to others. It was a problem of *growth*. We are told that 'the disciples were increasing in number'. But the problem was solved by the simple expedient of delegation. In fact the purpose of the so-called ministry today could be seen almost entirely in the training of shepherds, rather than in shepherding itself. Thus we see in Ephesians 4:11-12 that pastors are 'for the equipment of the saints for the work of ministry for building up the Body of Christ'.

Our present almost universal pattern of ministry, and its failure to sustain growth in the Church has been well brought out in the report *Divide and Conquer*.[17]

As numbers of people per parish rise, so the available pastoral care per person decreases. To start with the pastor simply gets busier, but he eventually reaches his work peak and from then on the pastoral function of the Anglican parish begins to break down. Pastoral care then becomes inevitably selective... Particular personality types may find a weakness in the pastor's defences and use it to gain a disproportionate amount of his time. *Care becomes geared* to crisis rather than promotion of growth... Meanwhile, the population at large finds the pastor occupied phrenetically with the chosen few... The retention of patterns of radical care based on one person per parish, whatever its population, strangles the growth of the church numerically, personally and corporately...and points to a pastoral mis-match between intention and action which demands reformation.

In other words, a church will never be a caring community and fulfil its pastoral role until it is able to share that pastoral responsibility amongst its members. It should never be left in the hands of one person or a small coterie of persons, but should be so organised that it expands its effectiveness as the church grows, and so caters for all in sufficient depth. The present use of the word 'discipling' to describe this work is an unfortunate one, but the principle behind it, which is to delegate pastoral responsibility so that it can be done effectively and not hinder growth, is a correct one, and certainly was the normal practice in the early Church.

The teaching role of the Church

There is some controversy as to whether pastoral and teaching are one ministry or two. The definite article is missing in front of the word "teacher" which would suggest that Paul is referring to "pastor-teachers", and that both roles are to be seen in one person. We have made it clear that in this part of the book we are not primarily concerned with "office", so that the question is an open one. Jerome, for example, felt that they should be regarded together. 'He who is a shepherd,' he wrote, 'must also be a teacher.' The Catholic theologian Joseph Brosch argues for separating the two,[18] whereas Eduard Schweizer takes an intermediate position, believing them to have been originally separate but to have come more and more to be linked in one person.[19] I agree with Arnold Bittlinger that it is not an important issue. One knows of men who are gifted teachers, but who flounder when it comes to pastoral matters. Equally one knows of brilliant pastors, who are inadequate teachers. All we need to say again is that *both* the pastoral and teaching ministry are essential for the well-being of the Church; that they may not always be found in one person, although they sometimes are; and that both roles are necessary in the leadership of the universal and the local church.

One has only to turn to the New Testament to see how important this ministry is. In this the Church was following in the best tradition of Judaism. Jesus Christ commissioned the Church both to 'make disciples of all nations' and to teach them 'to observe all that I have commanded you'.[20] The disciples refused to accept the ban placed on their teaching by the Pharisees, but 'did not cease teaching and preaching Jesus as the Christ'.[21] When Paul writes to Timothy he places gifted teaching high in the list of qualifications required of Christian leaders, and urges Timothy to fulfil his teaching ministry. All through the long history of the Church, teaching has been regarded as of prime importance, and episcopacy rose to its position of importance in church government because the Church needed norms for Christian teaching at a time when the Church was threatened by many heretical teachers. Bishops soon became the guardians and exponents of orthodoxy.

The evangelistic role of the Church

We have seen already how seldom the office of evangelist is mentioned in the New Testament. In fact, we only have the name of one person, Philip, who evangelised a city in Samaria (in Acts 8). But even he needed the assistance of the apostles Peter and John before his converts could become fully initiated as Christians. Nor do we see the apostles, as such, committed wholeheartedly to evangelism. When the persecution came to the Church in Jerusalem the apostles stayed where they were, and it was the laymen who were scattered throughout Judaea, and 'went about preaching the word'. One of these laymen was Philip. The truth of the matter is that the Church in its infancy does not seem to have gone in for specialist evangelists. The whole Church was evangelistic, although some would obviously have been more gifted than others, as in the case of Philip. Ever since, the Churches have been slow to recognise the ministry of evangelists. It was D. L. Moody, the American evangelist in the nineteenth century, who persuaded the Anglican Church to support its first full-time evangelist, the Revd. Hay Aitken, son of the Revd. Robert Aitken, who, though vicar of Pendeen in Cornwall, travelled with an apostolic ministry throughout Britain and was highly successful as an evangelist. William Booth, the founder of the Salvation Army, was so impressed by Robert Aitken that he sent his own son, Bramwell Booth, to learn about evangelism from him. But the Churches have probably been more right than wrong in not being enthusiastic about appointing full-time evangelists. It does not seem to have been a speciality the early Church went in for very much. The reason seems clear: the whole Church bore the burden and responsibility for evangelism. It did not pass the buck to someone else, certainly not to some individual separated from the Church. Our modern style of evangelist often justifies himself on the grounds of the comparative failure of evangelism in the Church today. But the argument is not a sound one. In fact, it can be another example of "office" discouraging rather than encouraging growth. While evangelists do the job for the Church, the Church itself will not be concerned about doing it properly itself. It is necessary that the whole Church fulfils its role in evangelism, even if the actual evangelism will tend to be concentrated in the hands of comparatively few people. What is needed is local church evangelism as part of the overall strategy of ministry in every church. There will still be a need for a few specialist evangelists (who ought themselves to be fully committed members of local churches), but the main weight of evangelism should be part of the regular life of the church, not an occasional whim or fancy of the minister. The Church today does not need evangelists; it needs to begin to be evangelistic. It cannot hope to grow unless it is deeply committed to evangelism in the area in which it is situated and to the furthest corners of the earth. It is not simply a matter of adding new members, although this is obviously essential, for without it there is no growth; it is also a matter of inward growth and maturity. For a church which does not give its life to others will utimately lose its life. There can be no maturity for a church unless there is at the same time a deep and active commitment to evangelism.

Having considered what ministry is all about in the New Testament, we need now to look to its perfect exponent, the Lord Jesus Christ, our purest pattern, and the source of its continuance in the Church, in the person of the Holy Spirit, who carried on where Jesus left off, and saw to it that Jesus's work would continue in and through his disciples.

4

The Divine Pattern

For the Son of man also came not to be served but to serve, and to give his life as a ransom for many. Mark 10:45.

WE HAVE SEEN something of the *scope* of ministry. We need now to turn to see its *pattern* in the ministry of the Lord Jesus Christ and the Holy Spirit. Jesus Christ in his earthly life set us an example, and his life and work are the most profound exposition of Christian ministry that we shall ever see. We need to look no further; Jesus, the Son of God, fulfilled perfectly all the roles we have so far mentioned. And that same ministry is to be continued *now* in the power of the Holy Spirit through the Church which is the Body of Christ.

Jesus the apostle

Jesus was 'the *apostle* and high priest of our confession' (Heb. 3:1). God loved the world so much that He sent His Son to save it. As someone has put it. 'God only had one Son and He was a missionary.' In the Incarnation the Son of God revealed the ultimate extent of the love of God — the total involvement in the creation he had come to save. No greater love has ever been seen before or since. 'Though He was rich, yet for your sake He became poor, so that by His poverty you might become rich' (2 Cor. 8:9). He surrendered his divine prerogatives and left the glory of heaven for the squalor of

earth. God moved, and so his Son was able to inaugurate an
apostolic Church.

Jesus the prophet

Jesus Christ was a true *prophet*. He was the very Word made
flesh (John 1:14). He not only spoke God's Word, *he was and is
God's Word to the world.* No wonder the woman at the well
cried out, 'Sir, I perceive that you are a prophet' (John 4:19).
No wonder the disciples on the road to Emmaus called Him
'a prophet mighty in deed and word before God and all the
people' (Luke 24:19). Some in the crowd on another occasion
said, 'This is really the prophet' (John 7:40). Jesus also told
His disciples how he prophesied. 'I have not spoken on my
own authority,' he said, 'The Father who sent me has himself
given me commandment what to say and what to speak. And
I know that the commandment is eternal life. What I say,
therefore, I say as the Father has bidden me' (John 12:49-50).
And again he said, '...the word which you hear is not mine
but the Father's who sent me' (John 14:24).

Jesus the pastor

Jesus was a superb *pastor*. In Hebrews 13:20, the writer
describes him as 'the great shepherd of the sheep'. Peter calls
him 'the chief shepherd' in 1 Peter 5:4. And Jesus took the
title to himself in John 10:11. 'I am the good shepherd. The
good shepherd lays down his life for the sheep.' You could
hardly have a better description of the pastoral role of the
church than that — to lay down [your] life for the sheep. If
taken seriously, it exposes one of the great weaknesses in the
Church, a lack of *self-sacrificial love for people.*

The famous high-priestly prayer of Christ, looked at from
one angle, is the Son's report to the Father of his pastoral
ministry. Jesus is giving an account of his stewardship. In this
prayer we see the main components of pastoral care:

   1. *Feeding*

Jesus was able to tell the Father, 'I have given them the
words which thou gavest me, and they have received them

and know in truth that I came from thee... I have given them thy word' (John 17:8, 14). He had 'made them to lie down in green pastures' and led them 'beside still waters'. The faithful disciples knew this. When many drew back and no longer followed Jesus, Simon Peter, acting as spokesman for the Twelve, said, 'Lord to whom shall we go? You have the words of eternal life' (John 6:68).

2. *Guarding*

Jesus was also able to report to the Father, 'While I was with them, I kept them in thy name, which thou hast given me; *I have guarded them*' (John 17:12). He was 'the door of the sheep' (John 10:7f). Those who entered by him were saved, and he laid down his life for the sheep.

3. *Praying*

'I am praying for them,' Jesus said (John 17:9). 'I do not pray,' he told the Father, 'that thou shouldst take them out of the world, but that thou shouldst keep them from the evil one. Sanctify them in the truth; Thy word is truth' (John 17:15). Jesus goes on to pray for their unity. The true pastor will pray for the sheep entrusted to him.

4. *Consecrating*

Most moving of all, Jesus told his Father of the dedication of his life for the sake of the people entrusted to him. The Living Bible translation draws out the meaning of this part of Jesus's prayer, and we can see how appropriate it is to the theme of this book. 'I consecrate myself *to meet their need for growth in truth and holiness*' (17:19). All ministry in the Church, whether it be the ministry of leadership or any other kind, needs to flow through people who are completely consecrated. Only dedicated leaders have the capacity to lead people 'in truth and holiness'. Only dedicated leaders will be able to instil dedication in others.

Jesus the teacher

Jesus was a great *teacher*. Although he had no human quali-fications, had secured no degrees, and so far as we know only received the most elementary education, he was gratuitously given the title "Rabbi" and told that he was "a teacher come from God" by none other than the high-ranking Nicodemus, himself a member of the Sanhedrin (John 3:2). Although on this occasion Jesus made no comment but took the conversation immediately to Nicodemus, at a much later date, shortly after washing his disciples' feet, he did accept this title. 'You call me Teacher and Lord,' he said, 'and you are right, for so I am' (John 13:13). There is no need to attempt to substantiate this, for the Gospels abound with references both to the actual teaching he gave, and to the reaction that people had to it. 'The crowds,' we read, 'were astonished at his teaching, for he taught them as one who had authority, and not as their scribes' (Matt. 7:29). Out of the Son of God poured forth the most sublime teaching the world has ever known. It drew large crowds of people, and has inspired millions ever since.

Jesus the evangelist

Jesus was a great *evangelist*. He earned for himself the title "friend of sinners", and those who gave it to him in derision had no idea at the time how much they were complimenting him! He declared 'the Son of man came to seek and to save the lost' (Luke 19:10). It is Luke who is at such pains to show that Jesus Christ is the great prototype of the true evangelist. In him the role of evangelism is most gloriously exemplified. He seems to have suffered from no communication problems, such as modern pundits write about in their evangelistic manuals. His life was dominated by compassion. He had a shepherd's heart as he looked out on the serried ranks of his listeners. 'When he saw the crowds, he had compassion for them, because they were harassed and helpless, like sheep without a shepherd' (Matt. 9:36). But even at that moment of truth, He knew that He would never be able to cope with such needs on his own. He asked the disciples to begin to pray for shepherds — 'pray, therefore, the Lord of the harvest to send out labourers into his harvest' (9:38). His compassion broke down the barriers, so that, even though the brief he had ᵣeceived from the Father had not included the Gentiles, nevertheless when the occasion presented itself he ministered to them. He seems equally at home in the company of Pharisees and harlots, Roman soldiers and Jewish collaborators, men and women, old and young. All came to him, and only the insincere and the hypocrites received his condemnation. He was the greatest communicator the world has ever known.

The ministry of the Holy Spirit

So we see Jesus as the true minister. We see his ministry in all its greatness as the pattern of our own. But how can ours possibly be like his? Jesus encouraged his disciples to believe that what he had done, they would also be able to do. Like the mother bird who pushes her fledglings out of the nest when the time has come for them to fly, so Jesus sent out first the Twelve, and then the Seventy, to heal and exorcise in his name. He was preparing them for the time, which was soon coming, when he was no longer going to be with them. He assured them that this was not going to be a disaster, but was for the best. 'The fact of the matter,' he told them, 'is that it is best for you that I go away, for if I don't, the Comforter won't come. If I do, he will — for I will send him to you' (John 16:7. Living Bible). Jesus assured them that it was going to be "business as usual" after his death. 'In solemn truth I tell you,' Jesus said, 'anyone believing in me shall do the same miracles I have done, and even greater ones, because I am going to be with the Father' (John 14:12. Living Bible). The answer to the problem was plain — the Holy Spirit was going to come and take over, and so continue the work of Jesus in the lives of all future generations of Christians. But we need to notice the significance of this principle, for it is of immense importance. William Temple, in commenting on the departure of Christ, writes:[1]

This hard saying states in its most signal instance the fundamental principle of true education. The task of the teacher is to prepare the pupil for the time of separation, which must come, so that the pupil may find within himself such resources as enable him to follow the direction in which the teacher has started him without any further aid. It is not only that the time of separation must come; it is a good thing that it should come, for otherwise that inward strength, which it is the purpose of education to develop, will never be exercised.

The significance of this is crucial. For if in this supremely important instance it was best for the Church that Christ should leave, and the Holy Spirit should come, so we shall find, as we look for principles of growth, that there will come those moments when dependence becomes a tyranny which stifles initiative and hinders growth. There will have to be many "leavings" so that Christians may learn to grow, and so that the educated become educators, and the sheep become shepherds. In all this the ministry of the Holy Spirit is vital.

If Jesus Christ's ministry is the pattern of ours, then we are not surprised when we see the same pattern in the ministry of the Holy Spirit. We see this when we examine Jesus's own teaching about the Holy Spirit in John 14-16. It is summarised in the words of Jesus about the Holy Spirit, 'He will glorify me, for he will take what is mine and declare it to you' (16:14). The Holy Spirit's role is not to depart from the pattern of Christ, but rather to work that pattern out corporately in the life of the Church.

The apostolic Spirit

Like Jesus Christ, the Holy Spirit is an *apostle*. Twice Jesus says that God will *send* the Spirit to them. 'But the Counsellor, the Holy Spirit, whom the Father will send in my name...' (John 14:26). And later Jesus reiterated this, 'I will send him to you' (John 16:7). The Holy Spirit is God's traveller, and when he comes he gives to God's people the travelling instinct or the pilgrim spirit. When he is quenched and grieved the Church will be motionless. When he is followed and obeyed the Church will move adventurously. The Holy Spirit is a most unsettling agency. he never allows us to stand still for long.

The Spirit of prophecy

The Holy Spirit is also the spirit of *prophecy*. As we read in 2 Peter, 'No prophecy ever came by the impulse of man, but men moved by the Holy Spirit spoke from God' (1:21). There is a fascinating statement by Christ about the work of the Spirit in John 16:13. 'When the Spirit of truth comes, he will guide you into all the truth; for he will not speak on his own authority, but whatever he hears he will speak, and he will declare to you the things that are to come.' As we have already seen, Jesus said of himself, 'I have not spoken on my own authority' (John 12:49). So Jesus sees the work of the Holy Spirit as the continuation of his own in the Church and the world. But we also see in John 16:13 that the Holy Spirit's prophetic ministry embraces all three of the elements we have seen in the ministry of the Old Testament prophets and of Jesus Christ. He is concerned with speaking forth, through God's people, the words of God. He is also concerned with foretelling the future, 'He will declare to you the things that are to come.' There is also more than a hint of that intuitive ministry of the Spirit. 'Whatever he hears he will speak.'

The pastoral Spirit

We also see that the Holy Spirit comes to *shepherd* or *pastor* the people of God. Jesus said, 'I will pray the Father, and he will give you another Counsellor [Gk. *paraclétos*], to be with you for ever... I will not leave you desolate' ('I will not abandon you or leave you as orphans in the storm' *Living Bible*) (John 14:16, 18). The Holy Spirit, literally, is the one who comes alongside to counsel us. What a glorious description of the Church's pastoral ministry! True pastoral ministry is sitting alongside a person, not arraigning him from a pulpit six feet above contradiction (and consideration). The Holy

Spirit gives to us the ability to sit where people are, and give them God's words and love.

The teaching Spirit

The Holy Spirit is also God's *teacher.* Jesus said of him, 'He will teach you all things, and bring to your remembrance all that I have said to you' (John 14:16). We have the Holy Spirit to thank for the New Testament, and the apostles and others for their faithful dependence upon him to remind them of all that Jesus had said. It is the Holy Spirit who inspires the mouth of the teacher, the ears of the taught, and the minds of both. Without the Holy Spirit there is nothing to teach, and without his help there can be no effective teaching in the Church.

The evangelistic Spirit

The Holy Spirit is also the divine *evangelist.* Jesus said about the Spirit, 'When the Counsellor comes...he will bear witness to me; and you also are witnesses because you have been with me from the beginning' (John 15:26-7). Luke shows us in both his Gospel and Acts how passionately the Holy Spirit evangelises, and how he instils His passion for the conversion of men and women into God's people. Again, Jesus told the disciples that it would be the Holy Spirit who would bring conviction to the world. 'And when he comes, he will convince the world of sin and of righteousness and of judgment; of sin because they believe not in me; of righteousness, because I go to the Father, and you will see me no more; of judgment, because the ruler of this world is judged' (John 16:8-10). Without the Holy Spirit the Church cannot succeed in its task of evangelising the world. It is the Holy Spirit who gives power to the Church so that it can fulfil its role of reaching the unbelieving and disobedient world around it.

The ministry of the Church

So the One who was God's apostle, sent by the Father into the world, now sends his apostles into the world. 'As the

Father has sent me, even so I send you' (John 20:21). And he breathes into them the Holy Spirit, and promises to send the same Holy Spirit to them; so, as Paul says, the ascended Christ from Pentecost onwards gave gifts to men — 'some apostles, some prophets, some evangelists, some pastors and teachers', for the express purpose that the Body of Christ might be built up and grow to maturity 'to the measure of the stature of the fulness of Christ' (Eph. 4:11-13). And the Spirit who was given to Christ "without measure" now flows freely through the Church, so that Paul could describe his ambition as that of presenting 'every man mature in Christ' (Col. 1:28). In Acts 20 we see in Paul's charge to the leaders of the Church at Ephesus how freely the Holy Spirit was at work in the apostle. Like Jesus in his high priestly prayer in John 17, Paul is giving an account of his stewardship. He had conscientiously taught them, not shrinking 'from declaring to you anything that was profitable' (20:20). He had declared to them 'the whole counsel of God' (v. 27). And he reminds them of their role. He had shepherded the elders, that they in their turn might be shepherds. 'Take heed to yourselves and to all the flock,' he tells them, 'in which the Holy Spirit has made you guardians, to feed the Church of the Lord' (v. 28). So we see again the principle working itself out, that the various spheres of ministry are gifts of Christ to equip Christians for the work of ministry. We minister, in other words, that those to whom we minister may themselves minister to others. So the Church grows. So leaders (like Paul) can be whisked away from the scene of action, and the Church goes on growing. It has within itself the secret of spontaneous expansion.

Although we are not concerned for the moment with "offices" — only with the five-fold operation of ministry in the Church — yet it is obvious that it is through people that these ministries flow. Sometimes people's gifts and aptitudes will tend to be concentrated mainly in one of these spheres. It is not too difficult to discover which kind of ministry a particular person has. A person who finds travelling easy, and

can adapt to different environments may be called to an
apostolic ministry. A person who knows how to listen to God
and hear his word, and who delights to spend much time in
his presence, may be called to a prophetic ministry. In our
strongly activist society we don't have too many people in this
category, and this is one reason for the dearth of the prophetic
ministry. An evangelist loves the world and is eager to share
the good news with it. He will know a good deal about it. The
prophet may not be too keen on reading the newspaper, but
the evangelist will often have his nose in it. He needs to know
a lot about the world he is in, for he has to understand how
people think, and be able to put his message in the words and
idiom that people will understand. The language of Zion will
not do. The pastor loves people, and knows how to get
alongside them, make them feel at ease, and bring God's light
to their problems. The teacher loves God's Word and truth.
He will be often reading it, and will also be gifted in
communicating it to others.

Of course, all these ministries need the anointing or charism
of God if they are to be effective. Natural abilities, however
dedicated they may be, should not be treated as substitutes
for spiritual abilities. It may often be true that more than one
of these ministries can be exercised in one person. In fact the
greater the responsibility in leadership, the more comprehensive will be the enabling. It is possible, for example, as in the
ministry of Christ, to discover all five elements strongly
evident in the ministry of an outstandingly gifted person. But
what is much more important is that we should expect to find
all these five elements in the leadership of each local church
which, according to the New Testament, should be a team
ministry. It is important to see that it was never intended that
there should be one man who is to be the fountain-head of all
spiritual ministry in the church. Ministry in the New
Testament was always team ministry. That it is far from
being so today is, alas, true. Men should be trained for the
ministry with this in mind. There are many ministers today
who cannot or will not team up with others. At least they can

say that neither were they trained for it, nor did the job specification include it. The whole mental attitude of ministers is conditioned to a lonely single-handed life, with the pattern of life only varied by the occasional arrival of an assistant, who can often be as lonely a person as the minister himself. Plurality of leadership was the norm in the New Testament, and so there was no excuse for loneliness. If it were adopted in principle today it would remove the need for those pathetic letters which lonely parsons wrote to Dr. Leslie Paul, when he was drawing up his famous report for the re-organisation of the Church of England's ministry. 'I am a prey to despair.' 'Mr. Paul, have you ever thought of suicide? I often have', and so on. This was never meant to be. The team ministry — by which I mean not only ministers of different churches teaming up together, but also, what is more important and practical, the chief minister sharing his ministry with other leaders, most of whom will be laity — should have within it all five spheres of ministry, and so should be competent to build up the Body of Christ. And as it functions properly it will itself be raising up more and more ministries as the church grows, so that growth can be sustained and not seize up. As David Sheppard has written, 'If we believe in working in teams, we need not wait for pastoral schemes.'[3] If a bishop knows how to cut through the red tape to do the essentials, so can anyone else!

5

The Apron of Humility

Put on the apron of humility,
Serve your brother, wash his feet,
That he may walk in the way of the Lord,
Refreshed, refreshed.

Kathleen Armstrong, *Sound of Living Waters*

THERE IS ONE word which the New Testament uses more than any other to describe ministry. It is the Greek word, *diakonia*, which is translated "service". It has been pointed out by Eduard Schweizer that the writers were not short of words and could have used several others. There was the word *arche* meaning "office" and its cognate *archon* meaning a "ruler"; there was *time*, a position of dignity; *telos*, complete power of office; *leitourgia* and *leitourgos*, meaning service for the gods; *hiereus*, a priest, and so on. These words are used rarely or not at all. Schweizer concludes:[1]

> In view of the large number of terms available, the evidence of the choice of words is unmistakable. Before there has been any theological reflection all the New Testament witnesses are sure of one decisive fact: official priesthood, which exists to conciliate and mediate between God and the community, is found in Judaism and paganism; but since Jesus Christ there has been only one

such office — that of Jesus himself. It is shared by the whole Church, and never by one church member as distinct from others. Here, therefore, there is without exception the common priesthood, *with us laity*. (Italics mine)

According to Hans Küng, 'The New Testament writings avoid secular terms relating to "office", precisely because they denote a relationship of domination.'[2]

All this becomes even more vivid when we see the use which the New Testament writers make of this word. Jesus used this word to summarise his own ministry (Mark 10:45). Paul refers to the ministry of the Holy Spirit as "service" in 2 Corinthians 3:8. The gifts of the Spirit are also designated "service" in 1 Corinthians 12:5. Paul used it to describe his own ministry (e.g. Col. 1:25, and 2 Cor. 6:4), and that of Epaphras (Col. 1:7) and Timothy (1 Tim. 4:6). Leon Morris comments:[3]

Christianity was no slick imitation of existing ecclesiastical organisations. It made no attempt to set up a hierarchy modelled on previously existing institutions. It was well aware of the kind of thing that was common in the world at large. But it preferred *diakonia*...to the grandiose ideas of the Gentiles. It took a term in common use for the most ordinary kind of service and made that its characteristic term for ministering.

One of the most hopeful signs in the midst of the distinctly depressing situation of the Christian ministry is the almost universal acceptance throughout the Church of the servant attitude. The phrase "The Servant Church" came into vogue in the 60s and was much used at the 1968 Assembly of the World Council of Churches at Uppsala in Sweden, and at the Lambeth Conference of Anglican Bishops. In Vatican II, likewise, there was a significant shift of emphasis. In the Constitution of the Church the nature of service is stressed, and over against the Council of Trent there is a change from the non-biblical term "hierarchy" to "church ministry" (*ministerium ecclesiasticum*). This is also reflected in the Agreed Statement on Ministry and Ordination issued in 1973 by the members of the Anglican/Roman Catholic International Commission. 'The Christian community exists to give glory to God through the fulfilment of the Father's purpose. All Christians are called to serve this purpose... The goal of the ordained ministry is to serve this priesthood of all the faithful.'

This emphasis is all the more important as a healthy corrective to other emphases. There is, for instance, the power syndrome which dominates the world and which is an ever present danger in the Church. Personal empire building has marred the character of the Church throughout its history. Ambitious men have distorted the image of ministry because they have ceased to have the attitude of a servant. Ministry can so easily become an excuse for domination, and power struggles frequently disrupt the leadership of the Church. Churches very easily divide into cliques, often headed by personalities, and the problem that Paul faced in Corinth has been repeated all too frequently.

This is particularly important within the charismatic renewal. At the same time as much of the Church was stressing the servant nature of the Church, charismatic people were seeing the Lordship of Christ and beginning to stress authority. There was no great harm in that, provided that the servant attitude was not forgotten. In more recent times some charismatics have been giving even more emphasis to what they call "discipling". But what is important to notice is that the New Testament carefully avoids using this kind of language to describe relationships between believers. Instead it uses the language of *service*. It is true that the charismatic renewal has, especially in the United States, brought Christians into a state of near anarchy, in that they have moved away from a disciplined commitment to their church without coming under any other kind of authority. But if the language of "discipling" is used in place of "serving", it will simply be a way of replacing anarchy with tyranny,

It is also a corrective to our present cultural emphasis on equality, which has been reflected in the campaign for social and sexual emancipation. There may be good in some aspects of modern liberation movements, but because they are built on humanistic rather than biblical foundations, we need to be constructively critical of them.

Egalitarianism at its worst is an attempt to debunk for ever the servant attitude. It is a move which is contributing to the destruction of our society. As Christians we need to face this threat with the positive rationale of "service", whilst making it clear, as the New Testament does, that this is not a synonym for "slavery". Service is God's way of releasing the individual, whereas slavery is man's way of destroying him.

The servant in the New Testament

There are several words translated "servant" in the New Testament. One is *oiketes,* meaning a domestic servant. There is also *huperetes,* used to designate an oarsman who rowed in the lower tier of a war galley, in other words a very ordinary seaman. But the two most important words, and those most frequently employed, are *doulos* and *diakonos.* If you include their cognates they are used about equally in the New Testament. Lord Ramsey of Canterbury, the former Archbishop of Canterbury, has distinguished carefully between these two words,[5] for when we talk about "the Servant Church" we need to know what we are on about. The word *diakonos* is a functional word, meaning a person who renders acts of service to other people, particularly waiting at table. When Jesus said, 'I am among you as one who serves' (Luke 22:27), he is using this word. But the word *doulos* is a "relationship" word. It means literally a "slave", one who is owned by another person, with no rights or independent status whatsoever. Thus Paul could speak of himself and Timothy as the slaves of Christ (Phil. 1:1), and of Christ himself, in the same epistle, as taking the form of a slave and becoming obedient unto death (Phil. 2:1-8). Sometimes Paul does refer to himself as the *slave* of others, especially when he is wanting to underline his comparative unimportance in the correspondence with the church at Corinth, which was in the grip of the nefarious personality cult (see 1 Cor. 3:5). But generally speaking the word *diakonos* refers to that *function* which should be descriptive of all ministry in the Church and by the Church, while the word *doulos* is used to describe that *relationship* to the Lord, which is total commitment without reserves of any kind.

The word *diakonos*, almost more than any other word, contains within it, according to William Barclay, 'the very essence of Christianity; and the basic distinction between the Christian and the non-Christian way of life'.[6] There is an interesting study of the word by Beyer in *The Theological Dictionary of the New Testament*, edited by G. Kittel. The whole concept of service was unacceptable to both the Jew and the Greek. Service to the Greeks was 'slavish and illiberal', and, since the Greek was an individualist, he never wanted to serve anyone, only to develop himself. Beyer says, 'For the Greek in his freedom and wisdom there can certainly be no question of existing to serve others.' As far as the Jew was concerned, in Christ's time there had been a slide from the loftier sentiments of the law. Service had become a method of gaining merit for oneself, and, in any case, was never to be given to unworthy causes. All this serves to underline the revolutionary nature of Christ's commitment to service, as we shall see later. As T. W. Manson has well put it, 'In the Kingdom of God service is not a stepping stone to nobility; it *is* nobility, the only kind of nobility that is recognised.'[7]

Jesus Christ as a servant

We have seen how the word *diakonos* characterises the Christian ministry more than any other single word in the New Testament. A. T. Hanson has written, 'If there is one word in the New Testament for the Christian minister it is *diakonos* rather than *presbuteros.*'[8] The stress in the New

Testament is on service rather than order, on what we do for others rather than what we tell them to do for us. In our permissive society there is a great temptation for Christians to over-react, and to become excessively authoritarian. To do so is to be out of character with the New Testament. Nowhere can this be seen more clearly than in the ministry of Christ himself.

Jesus was a self-confessed servant. In Mark 10:45 he said, 'The Son of Man has come, not to be served, but to serve and to give His life a ransom for many.' The words have become so familiar to us that we easily miss the punch line. In Jesus's day the phrase "Son of Man" was frequently discussed. It was a Messianic title. They were expecting the Son of Man to come at any moment. There was considerable speculation about the details, but on one thing everyone was agreed — the Son of Man was coming to receive homage from the nations, particularly of course the Romans whom the Jews loathed so much. Had not Daniel (7:14) prophesied that to the Son of Man, "the Ancient of Days", was to be given 'dominion and glory and kingdom, that all peoples, nations and languages *should serve him*'?

But Jesus changed the whole thing round, and caused consternation as a result! 'No,' Jesus in effect said, 'you're looking in entirely the wrong direction; the Son of Man has come to serve not be served.' On another occasion Jesus did something just as audacious. He linked the phrase "Son of Man" with *suffering* and *rejection* (Mark 8:31). Oscar Cullmann has commented, ' "The Son of man" represents the highest conceivable declaration of exaltation in Judaism; *ebed Yahweh* (the servant of the Lord) is the expression of the deepest humiliation. This is the unheard-of new act of Jesus, and he united these two apparently contradictory tasks in his self-consciousness, and that he expressed that union in his life and teaching.'[9] Michael Green, in his book *Called to Serve*, points out that the Aramaic word for "lamb" *talya* is also the word for "servant".[10] So we meet the servant in Jesus's words and actions wherever we turn. It was never far from his mind.[11]

Jesus had no time for status seekers. He publicly con-
demned those who 'love the place of honour at feasts, and the
best seats in the synagogues, and salutations in the market
places, and being called "Rabbi" by men' (Matt. 23:6-7).
Jesus forbade the pursuit of titles and honours. 'You are not
to be called "Rabbi",' he said, 'for you have one teacher, and
you are all brethren. And call no man your "Father" on
earth, for you have one Father, who is in heaven. Neither be
called "Masters", for you have one Master, the Christ. He
who is greatest among you shall be your servant' (vv. 8-11).
Jesus himself turned his back on all such clap-trap. Had he
wished to rely on status and titles, he had the greatest. But to
him, service was more important than honours and rewards.
Would to God the Church had followed his example more
closely!

But it is surely in the feet-washing incident, described to us
in John 13, that Jesus's servant role is most fully revealed. It is
all the more poignant that the disciples had, so far as we
know, just been debating who should be the greatest (Luke
22:24). It was not the first time they had been on this subject.
In Luke 9:46 we are told that they had a "dialogue" (Gk.
dialogismos) on the same subject. The King James version has
"a reasoning". Bonhoeffer, commenting on this passage,
writes:[12]

No Christian community ever comes together without this
thought immediately emerging as a seed of discord. Thus
at the very beginning of Christian fellowship there is
engendered an invisible, often unconscious, life-and-death
contest. 'There arose a reasoning among them': this is
enough to destroy a fellowship... Where is there a person
who does not with instinctive sureness find the spot where
he can stand and defend himself, but which he will never
give up to another, for which he will fight with all the drive
of his instinct of self-assertion? All this can occur in the
most polite and even pious environment.

But Jesus told his disciples that this kind of thinking was foreign to him. 'The Kings of the Gentiles exercise Lordship over them,' he said, 'and those in authority over them are called benefactors. But not so with you; rather let the greatest among you become as the youngest, and the leader as one who serves. For which is the greater, one who sits at table, or one who serves? Is it not the one who sits at table? But I am among you as one who serves' (Luke 22:24-7).

Who knows? It may well have been at this point that Jesus stripped off his clothes and washed the disciples' feet. If so, it was just about the most devastating riposte to their argument amongst themselves. Authority in terms of bossing people around was completely alien to Jesus's life-style. The only authority he was interested in was that based on service. On this particular occasion the slave who normally would have done this menial task had not shown up. The natural thing would have been for one of the disciples to have substituted. But each of them left it to someone else. All of them (Judas apart) would have happily washed *Jesus's* feet. But most of them would have had problems with their fellow disciples. Peter would have found it impossible to wash the feet of those proud social climbers James and John. And how could Matthew, the Jewish collaborator, serve Simon Zelotes, the revolutionary fanatic? In the end it was Jesus who washed their feet, even the feet of the one who was about to betray him.

We can learn much from the reactions of Peter. He was not the kind of person who hides his feelings. Impulsive by nature, he was for ever blurting out what he felt. He reveals for all to see the subtleties of human pride. Now it is pride more than anything else which is a major hindrance to ministry in the Body of Christ. It is this insidious enemy which stalks its prey and wreaks havoc in church after church. We see it here in all its ugliness. First, there was the pride that would not wash the feet of others. Peter was culpable with all the rest of his brothers. He was too concerned about his own position to demean himself before others. The loss of his dignity was too high a price to pay. But secondly, there was the pride that would not let Jesus wash his feet. 'You shall never wash my feet,' he said to Jesus (John 13:8). This is a more subtle form of pride, in which we will not accept help or service from others. It is a form of pride which will never allow itself to admit any need, which assumes a self-sufficiency which is a denial of the very heart of fellowship. Put these two forms of pride together and you destroy fellowship, which is a constant "give-and-take" kind of reciprocity or it is nothing at all. But Peter was to reveal all. There was yet a third form of pride. When he heard Jesus say to him 'If I do not wash you, you have no part in me,' he said to Jesus, 'Lord, not my feet only but also my hands and my head!' This surely reflected a love for our Lord, but perhaps an admixture, too, of pride and unwillingness to let the Lord choose his place and ministry in the Church, be that worldly ambition in a spiritual context, which leads to competitiveness and domination of those who are brothers and sisters in Christ.

So Peter shows us the sins which prevented all the disciples — and prevent us — from ministering to others as Christ did. The proud attitude which will not bend, and give from the heart; the equally proud attitude which will "not be beholden to anybody", an attitude which William Temple called "completely unchristian".[13] Literally Peter said to Jesus, 'You shall never wash my feet *to eternity.*' And William Temple adds this comment, 'Ah Peter, you have struck the right note there; for it is unto eternity that your Lord would cleanse you.' So, as Christians, we minister to one another, giving and receiving, and setting no limits to the amount of generosity we bestow on one another. We are very close indeed to the heart of what ministry is all about when we see our Master on his knees before his brethren, washing the dust and dirt off them. The attitude of the servant is always open-ended. It is to serve *and to be served.* Jesus washed the disciples' feet, but he allowed a woman of the streets to anoint and wash his (Luke 7:37). Peter never forgot what the Lord did for him. In later years he wrote to his fellow Christians, 'Clothe yourselves, all of you, with humility toward one another...' (1 Pet. 5:5). Was he thinking of Jesus's towel when he wrote those words? The Roman writer Suetonius describes how the Emperor Caligula 'was fond of making some of the senators wait at his table *succinctos linteo,* that is in the guise of waiters'. John Stott comments:[14]

> It was great fun to turn senators into waiters. It gave a tremendous fillip to his pride. He would never have dreamed of waiting on them. So too these disciples of Jesus. They thought of themselves as apostles not waiters, as masters not servants. It was for someone else to do the dirty work, not for them.

But Jesus did not act 'in the guise of a waiter'. He was the servant of all.

The apostles as servants

The apostles learned their lesson. They did not always agree. Peter and Paul had moments of serious disagreement. But the subject of 'who should be the greatest' was never on their agendas. Paul was conscious of the role of apostles as exhibits to the Church and the world. 'God has exhibited us,' he wrote in 1 Corinthians 4:9. But God had not put them on a pedestal. Rather they were 'last of all, like men sentenced to death'. He goes on, 'We have become a spectacle to the world, to angels and to men. We are fools for Christ's sake...we are weak...we are held in disrepute...we have become, and are now, as the refuse of the world, the offscouring of all things' (4:9-13). They were, in other words, treated by the world, and even sometimes by the Church, as poor exhibits. How far was Paul's attitude from our modern cult of human personalities! It was the false apostles who thought so highly of themselves, and deliberately promoted the personality cult, vying with one another as to which was the greatest. But Paul exhorted men to have the humble servant mind of Christ. He writes to the Philippians, 'Do nothing from selfishness or conceit, but in humility count others better than yourselves. Let each of you look not only to his own interests but also to the interests of others. Have this mind among yourselves, which you have in Christ Jesus... who made himself of no reputation' (Phil. 2:3-7 A.V.). If Jesus turned his back on a quest for "reputation" so should we all.

But this comes out with even greater clarity in Paul's controversy with the Corinthians. Paul was being denigrated by the false bombastic apostles, who were claiming superiority over him, and were jostling for the top positions and honours in Corinth. The carnally-minded Corinthians had fallen for all this, and the Church had become gravely divided into personality cliques. But Paul, in writing to them, shows his complete disdain of such an approach. Christian leaders are particularly vulnerable to flattery, and the Corinthians flattered some of their leaders as freely as they criticised Paul. As far as Paul was concerned, this was simply a demonstration of immaturity, and so he writes, 'What then is Apollos, what is Paul?' He is so anxious to show up this exaltation of men that he speaks disdainfully of Apollos and himself by using the neuter! He answers his own question in a most devastating fashion, '*servants*,' he says, 'through whom you believed, as the Lord assigned to each' (1 Cor. 3:5). Here he used the word *diakonos*. But in 2 Corinthians 4:5, in a similar context, he uses the word *doulos* — a slave. 'We preach...Jesus Christ as Lord, with ourselves as your servants for Jesus' sake.' John Stott comments, 'The excessive and misguided loyalty which they were giving to certain leaders was due to their false view of the ministry.'[15]

Ministry in the Church needs to be delivered from this false view. Those who are in prominence as Christian leaders need to be vigilant that they do not fall into this temptation. Jesus said of the Pharisees, 'They loved the praise of men more than the praise of God' (John 12:43). There is a story told about the late Pope John XXIII. While visiting a hospital, he was presented with a white skull cap. According to tradition he ought to have given them his cap in exchange. But Pope John was a man who was ready to part company with cherished traditions if he thought they were wrong. 'I will not give you my cap for two reasons,' he told the nuns gently. 'The first is that I have no wish to create need for a capmaker with nothing more to do than make caps for the Pope. And the second is that this sort of thing can lead you into idolatry and superstition.'[16]

We are all servants

Not every Christian is called to be a leader in the Church, but all are called to be servants. If Jesus Christ called himself a "servant", then it is a title none of us need spurn. We saw in the previous chapter that all ministry is to be "service", and we have seen how the word *diakonos* is used freely in the New Testament. In 1 Timothy 3:8f., Paul refers to an order of deacons, and there is evidence that by the time of Ignatius of Antioch, at the beginning of the second century, the classical three-fold ministry of bishops, presbyters and deacons had evolved. But even in 1 Timothy Paul uses the word "deacon" very loosely, for he calls Timothy a deacon (1 Tim. 4:6), while in 1:12 he uses the word to describe his own ministry! This all goes to show how the early Christians were much more concerned with function than with office. Michael Green has commented on Paul's use of the word in 1 Timothy, 'Nothing could demonstrate more clearly that the pattern of the servant was normative for *all* Christian ministry.'[17]

There are some who want to revive the perpetual diaconate in our own day. One of these is Cardinal Suenens, who spoke on this subject at Vatican II. He especially stressed the need for it in small communities living in a kind of modern *diaspora,* and for churches in anonymous suburbia, 'for whom it is necessary to restore some awareness of the Church as a family'.[18] In the same speech the Primate of Belgium said that he thought 'the good of the people is the decisive criterion.' Certainly this was the main impulse in Acts 6 when the seven were appointed to "serve tables" so as to allow the apostles to fulfil their function of preaching and praying.

Certainly the order of deacons needs either reform or painless euthanasia. Today it is used as a kind of probationary period for the presbyterate. This, at least in my personal opinion, makes ordination to the presbyterate an anti-climax. In the Roman Catholic Church it is a way of letting men, especially those who are married, do almost everything a priest can do without actually celebrating Mass. It is also a convenient sop to women who aspire to greater things. But there is another reason why the present might be the right time to abolish the diaconate altogether. It is such an urgent task that the whole Church should see itself in the servant role that it is a great pity that there should be attempts to revive the diaconate terminology, which should more properly be applied to the whole Church. We are not bound to reproduce everything that is contained in the New Testament. Some ministries were *ad hoc* arrangements to meet a contemporary need. It is true there were deacons, although references to them are very sparse. One of the most interesting ones is in Philippians 1:1, where they are mentioned with the bishops (a term which was synonymous with that of presbyter). Michael Green suggests that in view of the fact that this was a thank-you letter for money it is reasonable to see them as the trustees or treasurers who had organised the fund-raising.[19] It would be quite in order to see deacons as administrators in the church; but to ordain them, or to constitute them a separate order is both unnecessary and inappropriate. We shall be dealing later with the question of leadership in the Church, and this does seem to be the role of presbyters or elders, not deacons as such. The kind of need that Cardinal Suenens has in mind, which is likely to increase greatly as persecution grows in the Church and as society collapses outside it, is better met by appointing elders. Stephen Clark has indeed written a most interesting book which is a plea for accepting the role of "unordained elders", and he cites as his main example the ascetic movement in the fourth century, which was a charismatic movement itself, requiring a new kind of leadership.

Whatever we may say about a diaconate in terms of *office*, in terms of *function* all Christians are called to a perpetual diaconate. It is most important that we see all this in the context of our modern life. Before the French and Industrial Revolutions and the independence of the United States in 1776, the social life of Europe and the colonies was still largely hierarchically structured. In such a society it was comparatively easy to see a role for servants. Slavery was yet to be abolished, and even highly principled men could see nothing unchristian about it. 'The rich man in his castle, the poor man at his gate' had their lives ordered by the good Lord. But egalitarianism, and the great revolutions which swept away the *ancien régime*, set up a new society in which no one served anyone else. It is all the more important in view of this that the Christian Church rediscovers the role of the servant, whilst insisting that there is no servant class distinct from everyone else, and that service is not a midde-class excuse for exploiting the poor, or keeping them in their place.

In the book *The Jesus Family in Communist China* there is an account of the community called Ye-Su Chia-ting. When the Communists took over in China, many of them came to see how the Christians lived. They boasted of their great achievements. 'Among us there are no leaders,' they said, 'everyone is a comrade.' One day a typical group arrived and arrogantly shouted for the pastor. The author of the book, Vaughan Rees, happened to be present. 'I saw him in the distance,' he wrote, 'he was pushing the manure cart, and he pushed it right into their midst before someone said "here he is". The Communists had drawn back from the offensive cart. They then wanted to know how he could keep adequate discipline when he did such a menial job.'[20] The pastor, whose name was Chow-shin-ming, explained that since they were all equal, he, the leader, had the privilege of doing the worst jobs. Dietrich Bonhoeffer has written:[21]

The Church does not need brilliant personalities but faithful servants of Jesus and the brethren...The question of trust, which is so closely related to that of authority, is determined by the faithfulness with which a man serves Jesus Christ, never by the extraordinary talents which he possesses. Pastoral authority can only be attained by the servant of Jesus who seeks no power of his own, who himself is a brother among brothers submitted to the authority of the Word.

And Mother Theresa of Calcutta still cleans out the toilets in her community.

6

The Charismatic Dimension

The apostles did manifestly go forth as men moved by the Spirit to communicate the Spirit to others. This administration of the Spirit is the key of the apostolic work.
Roland Allen, *The Ministry of the Spirit*, p. 42

IT IS A fascinating thing that the word "charismatic" should have shot into prominence in both the religious and secular worlds at approximately the same time. For nineteen centuries *charisma* 'kept itself to itself in its neat, narrow cope of theological meaning', Philip Howard tells us in an article in *The Times.*[1] It was not until 1947 that the sociologist Max Weber discovered this Cinderella word and launched it on its career to stardom. It was first internationally applied to President Jack Kennedy — describing the almost religious aura of leadership cultivated by the White House at the time, though rather tarnished by subsequent revelations about the Kennedys. Weber used it to describe 'a certain quality of an individual personality by virtue of which he is set apart from ordinary men and treated as endowed with supernatural, superhuman, or at least specifically exceptional powers or qualities'. Etymologists and philologists have a well-known dislike for sociologists. Philip Howard berates Max Weber. 'Sociologists,' he writes, 'are notoriously careless with the English language as people who chose a name for their discipline that is a monstrous miscegenation of Latin with Greek might be expected to be. After the sociologists had sunk their dirty claws into *charisma*, the trendy mob followed.' The word is now used to describe celebrated personalities and those with personal magnetism, charm, glamour or sex appeal. Muhammed Ali was said to be charismatic. His defeated opponent Frazier was not. But Philip Howard demands, 'If it must be used in other contexts, the person to whom it is applied should be worthy of such a grand word.'

But just when the sociologists were launching the word, so too were Christians, for quite another reason, and with its original meaning. The word comes from the Greek New Testament, and was used to describe concrete manifestations of the grace of God. The root word *charis* means "grace", and so *charisma* means "a free gift". It is thus one of the most beautiful words employed to describe the Lord Jesus Christ. He was 'full of *grace* and truth' (John 1:14). Paul cries out in a moment of ecstasy, 'Thanks be to God for his inexpressible *charisma*' (2 Cor. 9:15). In the previous chapter he has told the Corinthians, 'You know the grace of our Lord Jesus Christ' (8:9), a statement he repeats in chapter 13:14. But Philip Howard is right — until the 1950s it was only used by theologians, and even rather sparsely by them and in a merely technical sense. The average Christian had never heard of the word, and most of those who had heard it regarded it as part of the gobbledegook of academic theologians, and thus incomprehensible to the layman. But in the 1950s it began to be used to describe the "pentecostal" renewal within the historic Churches. In many ways it was the ideal word, for there was a need to distinguish this movement from the separatist Pentecostal Movement. Thus a respectable word like "charismatic" was a godsend. It was different enough from "pentecostal", yet descriptive of what the Holy Spirit was doing, at the same time having a more staid ring about it. It was even academically respectable. When the Roman Catholic movement began in 1967 it was initially called "pentecostal", but the Roman Catholics soon embraced the word "charismatic" for much the same reason as their Protestant friends. Moreover, as we shall see, the word was freely used in Vatican II, which gave it a most useful kind of imprimatur. In these days "charismatics" are rather less sure of the value of the term. It may have served its purpose well in the early days of the movement when there was a stress on charismatic gifts. But now that the movement has matured and moved into other areas of renewal the cap does not fit the head so well, and some are even trying to drop it. But words like this are much harder to bury than they are to resurrect, and this one almost certainly has come to stay. People will always talk of the charismatic movement or renewal. Our responsibility is to see that the renewal deepens and widens as it sees and hears more clearly what the Holy Spirit is doing and saying.

It should not be the emergence of charismatic religion in our day which surprises us, but its comparative absence for so long in the Western Church. We regard as novel today experiences and actions which have been normal in other, and on the whole better, times in the Church's history. The Church's golden eras have usually been charismatic in some senses of that word. We need to go first to the Bible to see what we mean by this. We see Moses in the Old Testament as one of the first of many charismatic leaders. Some of them were in the centre of the life of the people of Israel. But most of them, like the prophets, lived and ministered on the periphery of the nation. They were often unpopular and reactionary voices. Like John the Baptist they were 'voices crying in the wilderness'. Some of them paid for it with their lives. The charismatic dimension was unstructured and in some senses uncatered for. It often arose at times of moral degeneration as a kind of underground church. God's people did not know how to cope with long-haired prophets with their strange behaviour and peculiar life-style. Nevertheless they were an authentic element in the Old Testament, and some of their writings we have today in the scriptures.

The charismatic dimension in the ministry of Christ

But when we come to the New Testament, the charismatic dimension moves into the very centre in the person of Jesus Christ, and is fused with all other elements. It is no longer an eccentric side-show for a few exclusive (and usually elusive) persons. It becomes a genuine and regular part of the life of God's people. Jesus was a charismatic. But unlike the prophets who came before him, he was also a teacher and a pastor. He lived amongst God's people. He ministered (and died) at the centre. He mixed freely with all kinds of people. Actually, as we shall see, he said more about the continuation of the charismatic element of ministry than he ever said about the setting up of a hierarchical structure for the Church. He certainly did not set (as some of the prophets did) the charismatic and the institutional against one another, but he quite clearly intended his Church to continue to be charismatic in the same way as he had been. 'He who believes in me will also do the works that I do,' Jesus said (John 14:12). Certainly the early Church took him at his word, and the Church in its better moments has continued to do so ever since.

In his book *Jesus and the Spirit,* Dr. James D. G. Dunn seeks to answer the question 'Was Jesus a charismatic?' In his conclusions he writes, 'Jesus' experience of God was of a supernatural power compelling him to speak and to act.'[2] Some theologians believe that the earlier traditions of Jesus were even more charismatic, but that some of these elements are not included in the Synoptic Gospels.[3] Dunn continues, 'Jesus' experience of God embraced non-rational as well as rational elements — *dunamis* to heal as well as *exousia* to proclaim, and he regarded both as valid and important manifestations of God's Spirit.'[4] The old Liberal idea of "Spirit" — *Zeitgeist* as they called it — is inadequate to describe what Jesus experienced. Rather we see in the life and ministry of Christ the Spirit as power — or, as Dunn suggests, charismatic Spirit and apocalyptic Spirit. 'Jesus' consciousness of Spirit is the eschatological dimension to Jesus' ministry which Liberalism missed.'[5] Rightly Dunn warns us

about repeating Liberalism's mistake by ignoring Jesus's consciousness of sonship, and over-emphasing his consciousness of
Spirit. Dunn writes, 'As He found God in prayer as Father, so
He found God in mission as power... It is the interaction of
sonship and Spirit that gives Jesus' ministry its distinctive
character.'[6] We shall find the same thing in our own ministry. It
is essential to hold these two strands together. A ministry which
is charismatic but lacks the consciousness of sonship, easily
becomes sensation-seeking and cranky. But sonship without
charisma becomes all too easily pietistic and individualistic. Jesus
held the two together in perfect harmony.

We see both these strands in the Old Testament messianic
passages. What Jesus did was to take both to himself. He saw
himself as the suffering servant of Isaiah, 'despised and
rejected by men...smitten by God and afflicted' (Isa. 53:3-4),
the person who would bring healing to the nation through his
sufferings. But Jesus was equally at home with the prophecies
that spoke of a triumphant Messiah. When he returned from
the temptations of the desert he read Isaiah 61:1-2 in the
synagogue of Nazareth and said to an astounded congregation, 'Today this scripture has been fulfilled in your hearing'
(Luke 4:21). This speaks of a ministry of liberation which to
Jesus was quite consistent with suffering and rejection. One of
the majestic features of the ministry of Christ was the way he
acted charismatically in a totally natural way, and refused to
allow his ministry to be used by himself or others prestigiously.
He made it clear that he was not out to make a name for
himself through the miracles that he did. He forbade publicity,
and on more than one occasion ran away from the crowd,
especially when he judged its mood was to elevate him into a
false and dangerous position. All this is consistent with his
clearly annunciated role as a servant. He did what he did to
serve others, not to improve his own status or to line his own
purse. It was compassion, not popularity, which motivated him.
It was obedience to the Father, not the blind dictates of
sensuality, which made him set sail on the sea of human need,
which in its turn took him to crucifixion. Jesus brought the

charismatic dimension of ministry into the centre from the wild
and woolly extremes, and was himself the pattern charismatic.

The charismatic dimension in the early Church

The Church took the torch from the hands of Christ without
question. For them the work of the Holy Spirit was essential for
effective ministry. They obediently waited until the promised
Spirit filled them at Pentecost. Jesus baptised them in the Spirit
himself. Jesus also made it clear *why* he was going to baptise
them in the Spirit. 'You shall receive power,' he promised them
'...and you shall be my witnesses' (Acts 1:8). Their new
ministry began on the very day the Spirit came upon them. The
apostles began to minister in the power of the Holy Spirit. Peter
preached and 3,000 people were converted and baptised. The
apostles began to teach and pastor the people. There was the
Lord's Supper. They prayed together. They shared their lands
and property. The Holy Spirit launched the ministry, and Jesus
now gave, through the Spirit, his gifts to men, 'apostles,
prophets, evangelists, pastors and teachers'.

The New Testament makes it very clear that, just as the Lord
Jesus Christ derived his power and authority for his ministry
from the Holy Spirit, so did the early Church. There is no more
striking passage on this than in 2 Corinthians 3 and 4. In chapter 3 Paul shows how much superior the ministry of the Spirit is
to that of the law. 'The written code kills,' he says (v. 6). It not
only kills, but it condemns (v. 9). In contrast the Spirit "gives
life" and conveys righteousness. The period of the law was a
temporary one — a fading glory. But the age of the Spirit is
permanent, and brings an unfading glory with it. Moses had to
veil his face because he knew that the glory he had through his
encounter with God was only temporary. It was going to
disappear quickly (v. 13). But with us it is different. 'We all
with unveiled face,' Paul writes, 'beholding the glory of the
Lord, are being changed into his likeness from one degree of
glory to another' (v. 18). The gift and blessing of the Spirit is
not meant to come and go. It is God's will that we know that
blessing at all times.

It is not surprising, therefore, that in chapter 4 Paul lists the blessings which flow from this ministry of the Spirit. The first is — *encouragement* — '*We do not lose heart*' (v. 1). After the resurrection Peter went back to fishing. After Pentecost he began to do what he has been called to do — fish for men, and he landed a huge catch of 3,000 people at his first attempt! There are so many of God's people who have 'lost heart'. Is it not because they have forgotten the presence and power of the Spirit, or even never experienced him fully in their lives?

The second is — *honesty* — '*We have renounced disgraceful underhanded ways,*' Paul goes on. The Holy Spirit wants to make us open-faced and straightforward. He does not honour those who are devious and deceitful. If our ministry is under the control of the Spirit, we don't need to indulge in gimmicks.

The third is — *integrity* — '*We refuse to practise cunning or to tamper with God's word.*' Without the Holy Spirit there are many problems when we come to God's word. We are forced to "tamper" with it. We have to explain parts of it away. There are those parts which are outside our experience. We are strangers to them. But when the Spirit is in control we can let God's word speak for itself. We need not be ashamed of it, or be "cunning" in expounding it. No wonder Paul says that it is "by the mercy of God" that we have been given this ministry. Thank God we do not have to minister according to a set of rules. No, God has written his new law of love and grace 'with the Spirit of the living God...on tablets of human hearts' (2 Cor. 3:3).

Throughout the New Testament there is an emphatic link between ministry and the Holy Spirit. The apostles were 'filled with the Holy Spirit' for their ministry. Immediately after Jesus had commissioned them in John 20:21, we are told that he 'breathed on them', and said to them, 'Receive the Holy Spirit.' In Acts 6:3 when the Twelve asked the Church to choose seven men for the ministry of caring for the widows, they were to be 'full of the Holy Spirit'. The first martyr, Stephen, was 'full of the Holy Spirit' at his death (Acts 7:55). In 1 Corinthians 12 the gifts of the ministry are described as "spirituals". It was the Holy Spirit who said, 'Set apart for me Barnabas and Saul' (Acts 13:2). James Dunn writes, 'The earliest Christian community was essentially charismatic and enthusiastic in nature, in every aspect of its common life and worship, its development and mission.'[7] He goes on to show what a vital link there was between the Lord Jesus Christ and these experiences of the early Christians. Dunn writes, 'Even at this early stage Jesus was understood not merely as a sort of archetypal Christian charismatic, but religious experiences of the earliest community, including experiences like those enjoyed by Jesus himself, were seen as dependent on him and derivative from him.'[8]

In fact Luke links his gospel closely with the Acts. In the gospel, he tells Theophilus, he has recorded all that Jesus 'began to do and to teach' (Acts 1:1), the implication being that in Acts he is going to record that which Jesus *continued* to do and to teach, this time by the Holy Spirit through the disciples. Just as Herod, when he heard about the miracles that Jesus was doing, thought that John the Baptist had come back from the grave, there must have been many people who thought it was Jesus actually in the flesh at work through the early Christians. Of course, in one sense they were right. Jesus was alive. But it was the Holy Spirit who was continuing the divine mission of the Son through the Church which was his Body.

James Dunn's conclusion is that Jesus was not an ecstatic. 'He did not attempt to stimulate ecstasy or work up inspiration.' *But He was a charismatic.*[9]

He was charismatic in the sense that He manifested a *power* and *authority* which was not his own, which He had neither achieved nor conjured up, but which was given him, his by virtue of the Spirit/power of God upon him. The *power* did not possess him and control him so that He was its instrument willing or unwilling. But neither was He the author of it; nor was He able to dispose of it or ignore it at will... The *authority* was not his by academic merit or social standing; He had not earned it as a right. And yet it set aside all other authority however sacrosanct, and claimed a hearing before all others, for it came directly from his relation to God, immediately from his insight into God's will.

In the same sense as this superb summary of James Dunn's, the Church of Jesus Christ is meant to exercise *power* and *authority*. It is in the measure in which as Christians we are dedicated to God and filled with the Holy Spirit that we shall know this same power and authority in ministry. The charismatic dimension is essential if the Church is to function properly and effectively today.

The history of the Church since those early days makes sad reading. Again and again the charismatic dimension has been suppressed or has degenerated into heresy, fanaticism, and schism. One of James Dunn's main contentions is that Paul tried to grapple with the tension within the charismatic community between institution and order on the one hand, and *charismata* and freedom on the other. He believed that both could and should exist side by side, complementing not competing with each other. But, Dunn's argument continues, the evidence of the post-Pauline situation is that 'there is little place either for Lucan vitality or for the Pauline vision... The living voice of prophecy... has been all but stifled...and there is already a great risk that the tradition will become a strait-jacket with the Spirit imprisoned within office and institution.'[10] Dunn then suggests that John's was a last attempt to take the Church back to the Pauline ideal. Whether this is so or not, the institutional aspect of the Church more and more received emphasis, with the result that the charismatic aspect was neglected and the Spirit quenched. But the Church has never lost that tension, and the charismatic renewal of today is only one of many movements from Montanism onwards which have sought to redress the balance, and restore a truly charismatic dimension to the life of the Church. In his final remarks James Dunn regards this as 'the biggest challenge to twentieth-century Christianity'. We need, he says, 'to be open to that experience of God which first launched Christianity and to let that experience, properly safeguarded as Paul insisted, create new expressions of faith, worship and mission at both individual and corporate level'.[11]

The charismatic dimension today

Today there is a growing awareness and open-ness to this, and a real desire to allow the free and spontaneous expressions of the Spirit to manifest themselves alongside and closely related to the institutional expressions of life. Vatican II was careful to point out that these two elements should never be set against each other, but should be held together in constructive tension. For Roman Catholics the institutional aspect of the Church is as much a *charisma* as the charismatic. God gives both order and freedom, structure and spontaneity. During the Council discussion on October 22nd, 1963, Cardinal Suenens made his now famous intervention, disagreeing with Cardinal Ruffini who had wanted to limit charismatic gifts to the clergy. The Primate of Belgium made it clear 'that these special gifts of the Holy Spirit to the Church do exist today' and that it was wrong to limit the gifts either to the hierarchy or to the laity. 'The Church is a spiritual reality...for since the first Pentecost, the Church has existed and functioned under the direct influence of the Holy Spirit.' He went on to stress the need to develop the importance of the charisms and to *show the harmony between the charismatic and ministerial structures of the Church*. He concluded by saying, 'Without the shepherds the Church would be undisciplined; but without the charisms, it would be sterile. Therefore the pastors must heed the warnings of St. Paul and take care not to "stifle the Spirit".'[12] If ever a door were opened, this was the moment. Four years later the Roman Catholic charismatic renewal began in Notre Dame University in South Bend, Indiana, and Duquesne University in Pittsburgh, Pennsylvania. But the door was first re-opened in

Rome in 1963. Brother Gabriel Murphy, writing about Vatican II, described it as 'a plan for the rejuvenation of the Body of Christ in which the spiritual gifts of the Spirit have the capital role to play, especially in an upsurge of activity among the laity'.[13]

Other Churches have been much slower at seeing the charismatic dimension. Vatican II recognised something important and is helping to bring a new balance within the Roman Catholic Church. The Lambeth Conference, which is a gathering of the bishops of the world-wide Anglican communion, met in 1968, but did not have this matter on its agenda. The Agreed Statement on Ministry and Ordination by the Anglican and Roman Catholic Churches does stress the Holy Spirit in a number of important places. 'All ministries,' it states, 'are used by the Holy Spirit.' The qualification for exercising such a ministry 'is the gift of the Spirit'.[14] But it is a pity that "charismatic" is not included. The Vatican Council used this word or the word "charism" to describe this element in ministry. The trouble with a sentence like 'ministry is the gift of the Holy Spirit' is that it is both obvious and nebulous. The Church has been far too unspecific about the work of the Holy Spirit. The word "charismatic" does for the work of the Holy Spirit today what it did in the New Testament: gives it concreteness and removes the vagueness. For too long there has been a fatal assumption that the Church is being led and inspired by the Holy Spirit. But the word "charismatic" is arresting and startling. It suggests a new definiteness. It need not necessarily be associated with the charismatic renewal itself. After all, the Roman Catholic renewal did not start until Vatican II had concluded, yet the word was being used in the Constitution Lumen Gentium and there was a full discussion on the place of charismatic gifts in the Council several years before the new movement had started in the Roman Catholic Church. Protestant Churches have always been more vague about the Holy Spirit than both the Roman Catholic and the Ortho-dox. It has been one of their chief weaknesses. Alas, there is still little evidence that any of these Churches realise the extent of this malaise, or is taking any concrete steps to overcome this unfortunate imbalance.

If the Roman Catholic Church has been guilty of quenching the Spirit by over-emphasising the hierarchy, Protestants have done the same thing by over-emphasising the Word. Cardinal Suenens in his book *A New Pentecost*[15] quotes the Protestant theologian Jean Bosc:

> To isolate the Spirit from the Word is...dangerous — that is if I refuse to allow any dialectic between the two. This can lead to a kind of illuminism, which invests the most human of thinking with enthusiasm. It can lead to deviations, movements which are all emotion and no content, or to a fascination with relevance which refuses on principle to accord to the Word any kind of permanence within created reality. If the champions of orthodoxy, who rally to the Word, deny the Spirit, the pneumatics who appeal to the Spirit for the justification of every form of spiritual anarchy, are no better. The history of the Church, both universal and protestant, can provide, one after another, examples of this kind of imbalance.

The Church is committed to the ever-agonising task of creating and sustaining a healthy balance between the two. Cardinal Suenens has described the dilemma as 'finding the necessary bond between institution and liberty'.[16] He goes on:

> But we do not have to invent this bond: it is not of human making nor does it result from an agreement we negotiate among ourselves. This bond has a personal name: the Holy Spirit. He, by nature is the 'bond of unity', the creator of communion...who animates the entire Church from within, and it is the same Holy Spirit who gives to the Church the visible means and mechanisms of its structure.

So structures and life are both the gift of the Spirit. They are partners, not competitors.

The word "charismatic", as we have seen, arrived on the religious and secular stage at about the same time. But there is a world of difference between the two uses of the word. The covers on the final two issues of *Time* magazine for 1975 illustrate this point perfectly. The 22nd December cover had on it the pugnacious face of the late J. Edgar Hoover, head of the American FBI. The 29th December issue had for its cover the frail emaciated face of Mother Theresa of Calcutta. In the secular sense one would apply the word "charismatic" to Edgar Hoover; in the religious sense one could equally apply the term to Mother Theresa. But oh the world of difference between the two! A man wrote to *Time* magazine thanking them for their feature on twentieth-century saints, 'I realise now the difference between me and them. I get emotional, saints get involved.'

It is not easy to define what we mean by *charisma* when applied to Christians. Certainly we can reject the Max Weber secular definition that it has anything to do with personality or sex appeal. But it is important that we attempt some kind of assessment, for it is crucial to our understanding of how the Church functions. We have already said that all members of the Body of Christ are called to minister to one another. In that sense every Christian has a *charisma*. But what is this? If it is not personal magnetism that compels attention, neither is it saintliness. All Christians are called to be saints. Saintliness, properly understood, is conformity to the character of Jesus Christ. No Christian can duck out of that. But we are still no nearer to defining *charisma*. It certainly is not natural or human gifts, which may or may not be dedicated to Christ and useful for ministry in the Church. For instance, it does not follow that an admiral, who has brilliantly commanded an aircraft-carrier, has *ipso facto* the *charisma* of leadership in the Body of Christ, for the simple reason that the Church is not an aircraft-carrier! It may well be that such a man's gifts and training may be useful in the Church, but we dare not assume this. The trouble with much lay leadership today is that this assumption has been made far too frequently, with the result that the Church has been run as if it was a bank, or a department of the civil service, or a regiment in the army, or an aircraft-carrier.

Perhaps the word *charisma* could be defined as, *the sovereign gift of God the Spirit to a man or woman to be and to do what he has called them to be and to do in service to the Body of Christ and the world.* It is the divine equipping of someone for a task of ministry in the Body of Christ. Normally it is conspicuous, so that the Church is able to recognise and accept it, and commission or ordain that person for the ministry for which he has received such an anointing. It is both power (*dunamis*) and authority (*exousia*). The person may be unaware of it himself. If he is humble, he will certainly not press his claims for recognition. It is important to stress the divine aspect of *charisma,* especially at a time when the Church tends to stress the human aspect. In other words, we need to assert that God chooses whom he wills and that he equips them and authorises them. The Church has a part to play too, but the Church can only authorise those whom God has authorised, and can only recognise those whom God has gifted and empowered. No amount of theological training or human pressure can bestow *charisma* on a person. It is the sole gift of God, who gives it sovereignly to whom he wills, and when he wills. Thus it was the Holy Spirit who said, 'Set apart for me Barnabas and Saul for the work to which I have called them.' But the Church recognised what God had said and done and 'laid their hands on them and sent them off' (Acts 13:2-3). *Charisma* cannot be learned nor can it be bestowed by man. The Church is utterly dependent on the Holy Spirit, and without *charisma,* however learned ministers may be, however dedicated and however many of the right hands have been laid on them, their work will be a failure. Much of the Church has yet to learn what this means, and its failure to honour the Holy Spirit is one of the main reasons why it has ceased to grow. The charismatic dimension is a crucial factor in the renewal of the ministry of the Church today.

Part II

The Church and its Members

7

The Church and the churches

IT IS IMPOSSIBLE to deal adequately with the subject of Christian ministry without also dealing with the subject of the Church. It is equally impossible to do justice to the subject of the Church in one chapter. It really requires a book on its own. Nevertheless something has to be said, for ministry is for the benefit of the Church, not the Church for the ministry. The Agreed Statement on Ministry and Ordination produced in 1973 by the members of the Anglican-Roman Catholic International Commission makes this clear. 'The goal of the ordained ministry is to serve the priesthood of all believers.'[1]

One of the most important results of Vatican II was the clear enunciation of this principle. Some have called this change in emphasis "a Copernican revolution". In the *Lumen Gentium* Constitution the original order was: chapter 1: the Church as a mystery; chapter 2: the Church as a hierarchy; chapter 3: the Church as the people of God. Cardinal Suenens has described how the change took place:[2]

> Someone then proposed to me (I was the relator) that the order of the chapters II and III be inverted. I accepted the suggestion... Now I discover... that it was the genius of the Holy Spirit that changed the order of these chapters and thus brought to the forefront the reality that the Church is the people of God together: all the baptised living together in co-responsibility. Then there is the hierarchy made up of some of these people of God dedicated to a particular service of the rest.

At first sight it all appears perfectly obvious. But in actual fact it needs to be clearly stated in our day. All those who are set apart from others for any particular ministry in the Church are separated for the sake of the Church and its service and well-being, not for their own spiritual benefit, and certainly not to fulfil their own egos. Men and women are called by God to serve others, not to be served by them. There is no place for domination of people in the ministry of the Church. What authority there is, and Christ did delegate it, is the authority of service, not tyranny.

When we turn to the teaching of our Lord Jesus Christ we notice how little he says about the Church he came to found. As the founder of a world-wide society, which was to embrace all nations and races, he would, you would have thought, have laid down many clear regulations and guide-lines as to how the Church was to be governed, and who was to do what. Instead we find such laws conspicuous by their absence. We can learn a great deal from this silence. Jesus was concerned with principles of growth (hence his remarkable parables of the Kingdom) rather than with setting up a kind of spiritual bureaucracy to run the Church he knew he had come to build. He instinctively knew that *function* was more important than *office*. He knew that in the dangerous times that lay ahead the Church would have to be flexible in its style of ministry. It would have to adapt itself to many changing circumstances. So a book of rules would be useless. It would have incarcerated the Church and turned it ultimately into a sect of the Pharisees, for ever strangled by its own casuistry. But his silence also betokens a most moving trust he had in his disciples and in the Holy Spirit's power and authority which he was going to give to them. Since the Holy Spirit would lead them into all truth, he (Jesus) did not need to tell them everything. Thus ministry evolved slowly but surely in the early years of the Church, rather than being imposed by rules and regulations. That the Church down the cent-uries has attempted to impose laws rather than operate under the impulse of timeless principles has been the cause of much of its failure and present paralysis. But that such attitudes are at last changing fundamentally can give us considerable hope.

As is well known, Jesus only used the word "Church" (*ekklēsia*) twice, and in so doing gives us the clue to the most basic and vital distinction between the Church and the churches. In Matthew 16:18-19 Jesus said to Peter, 'And I tell you, you are Peter, and on this rock I will build my church, and the powers of death shall not prevail against it. I will give you the keys of the kingdom of heaven, and whatever you loose on earth shall be loosed in heaven.' We shall leave aside for the moment the question of the authority which Jesus here gave to Peter. But Jesus clearly had in mind here the universal Church, which was to stretch down the centuries and span heaven and earth. It was to be built on rock, not sand, and so it would survive all the assaults that would be made upon it. But in Matthew 18:17 Jesus has another aspect of the Church in mind. He is speaking about the situation when one person sins against another, but refuses to listen either to him or to others whom he might bring with him. In such a situation the final step is to 'tell it to the church'. Here Jesus has in mind a local gathering of people. It would be impossible and obviously inappropriate to share our personal difficulties with the universal Church! So we see here the local church, a homogeneous body of people with some kind of structure and identity.

This simple distinction between the universal Church throughout the world and throughout time and eternity, and its local manifestation has been obscured until recently. Partly this has been due to the emergence of denominations, some of which have denied the reality of the former concept of the Church, except in terms of invisibility, and most of whom have affiliated themselves into organisations which are smaller than the universal Church, but greater than the local one, while in the Roman Catholic Church the local church has tended to be overshadowed by the sheer bulk and weight of the universal Church. But Vatican II has gone a long way to correct this and to restore the local church to its importance. Cardinal Suenens writes about this:[3]

> Though Paul spoke about the Church of Corinth or Ephesus or elsewhere, he still used the singular church, when speaking of the total reality in this world. That is, the mystery of the church, the Church of God, is a unity in its very origin and at the same time it is a plurality. *It is a union of communities bound together and sharing in the one reality which they together make up.* We must not be afraid of plurality because plurality and unity are both essential dimensions of the church.

We have heard a lot about so-called "local church autonomy", the *right* of each local church to govern itself. But the language of "autonomy" is foreign to the spirit of the New Testament. Ministry and authority in the early Church were not thought of in terms of rights but rather of responsibilities. Jesus told his disciples not to lord it over one another as the Gentiles did. They were to serve one another. The whole notion of 'Don't you interfere in our church affairs' was alien to Christian thinking. There was a mutual sharing between churches on the basis of love. Any thought of local competition between churches was obnoxious to the New Testament principles of care and concern. It should be equally unthinkable that any person would be free to interfere in the internal affairs of any church of which he is not a really committed member. We shall be considering later the question of the authority of apostles and bishops, who had a ministry to several or many churches.

Independency is still regarded by some as the right form of church government. But this view is based on a false premise. It is assumed that the local church appears like Melchizedek — without parents. But that is, generally speaking, untrue. It comes into existence through the witness and work of another congregation. Independency is a middle-class heresy. We are all dependent on one another, and this is as true of each church as it is of each individual Christian within that church.

There is a further matter which needs mentioning. When we think of world evangelism, it calls for organisation and strategy, which are impossible for a single church, or even a few local churches. The needs of effective and well-integrated evangelism demand a close relationship between local churches. Local churches should not simply be selfishly concerned with their own affairs. They need to be willing to co-operate with, if necessary, many other churches in the planning and activity of evangelism.

When we turn from the gospels to the epistles we find an almost total absorption in the local church. Paul when he writes to the church in Corinth, tells it that it is "the body of Christ" (1 Cor. 12:27). In the same epistle he refers to the ministries which God has appointed *for the local church*. But we also notice a development in the thinking of Paul in his later epistles. The key one, of course, is Ephesians. Several scholars have questioned the Pauline authorship of Ephesians, mainly on the grounds of the more advanced teaching which it contains concerning the Church, saying that it suits more the period of Ignatius at the beginning of the second century. This is not the place to debate this issue. Let it suffice to say that it would seem to limit the revelatory ministry of the Spirit if it is assumed that the apostle Paul's view of the church, which in his earlier epistles is taken up largely with local church affairs, could not have been enlarged by further revelation, especially when the growth of the Church almost demanded it.[4] But what we do see in Ephesians, whoever is the author, is a truly Catholic concept of the Church, universal as well as local. The Church is 'the fullness of him who fills all in all' (1:23). It is the 'household of God', and it is built on the foundation 'of the apostles and prophets, Christ Jesus himself being the corner stone' (2:19-20). The Church is a "structure" (*oikodomē*) and 'grows into a holy temple in the Lord' (2:21). It is 'through the Church' that God's wisdom is to be made known (3:10) and his glory seen (3:21). There is only one body (4:4), and the ministry is for building it up (4:12). Husbands are to love their wives 'as Christ loved the Church and gave himself up for her' (5:25). Christ nourishes and cherishes the Church (5:29). All these quotations, whilst including each local church, obviously extend the scope of it to embrace God's people throughout the world, at that time spreading slowly but surely through the society of the Roman Empire. So we can see that the five-fold ministry, which we have already discussed, of apostles, prophets, evangelists, pastors and teachers, has a much wider application than the ministry we see outlined in similar terms in 1 Corinthians 12. This leads us to make our second conclusion. The first was that the ministry exists for the church, not the church for the ministry; the second is that the ministry exists for the local church *and* for the universal Church. In other words, God provides those who can minister to the needs of God's people in the local church, and others whose ministry is to the wider Church.

We shall be considering in chapter 10 whether we can find in the New Testament a blueprint for the Church's ministry for the rest of history. But we do need to see the Church in both its historical and its eschatological perspectives. We cannot simply dismiss the past and start all over again, neither are we to be bound conservatively to the past or the present. We need a vision before us of the eschatological hope of the Church, the bride adorned and ready for her husband. We need both a respect for the past and an unwillingness to opt out of our continuity with it, right back to the apostles, and also a vision which will for ever deliver us from complacency and make us ready for all the pain and unsettlement of change. *America* magazine has called this burrowing back into the past for the "perfect church" — be it in the first century or the Reformation or whichever our favourite period may be — "primitivism". Cardinal Suenens calls it "an archeological expedition".[5] The same magazine has called the opposite "presentism", when we consider the present moment as the only reality. The Church lies somewhere along the direct route from Pentecost to the Parousia. We are permitted glances backwards, for there is a continuity with the past. We can also look ahead and see what the Church is meant to become. The one thing we must not do is to be beguiled into Church perfectionism — the notion that some great day is coming when the Church (normally it is ours!) will be perfect. We must not suffer from any such illusions.

At the start of the Church's pilgrimage through the centuries it is obvious that the chief focus was on the local church, with a variety of ministries and functions, and with a simple structure and order. But as the Church grew in size, and spread further and further out from Jerusalem, and as on the one hand the apostles one by one died, mostly as martyrs, and on the other hand dangers increased, especially from heresies such as Gnosticism, sectarian movements like Montanism, and the increasingly hostile reactions from the Roman Empire, so necessity created a new order, what we call today episcopacy, a supra-local authority and focus of unity for the scattered Christian communities. It was both natural and inevitable that the concern and need for pastoring should have created the need for ministry which would be more comprehensive than local church ministry, and would be the means of uniting the churches in any given area, and on a larger scale the churches in provinces, countries and ultimately the entire world.

There was another factor that needs to be mentioned here. The New Testament canon was not finalised until the fourth century, and not without some controversy. In the long interim period there needed to be some norms of orthodoxy, as there were many strange apocryphal gospels circulating, as well as a growing number of Gnostic writings. The apostles were obviously the custodians of orthodoxy, but when most of them had died there was a growing need felt for those who could unite the churches and help with the growing number of doctrinal issues which were coming up. That episcopacy was the result is a well-established fact. But the important thing at this stage is to notice that the ministry within the local church was not felt to be sufficient to deal with these larger issues and so the need for a ministry to the universal or catholic Church was created.

But it is the denominations which complicate all this. Juan Carlos Ortiz has written:[6]

> The problem is that in recent centuries a new type of church has appeared, a church that is neither universal nor local. It's bigger than local, and smaller than universal. It is the denomination. The denominations have tried every form of government... The problem lies in the fact that there is no biblical precedent for denominationalism... So long as we cling to the old wineskins of our denominations, we will not move ahead with God.

But in any case should we necessarily be looking for the exact pattern in the New Testament? And is there such a pattern there anyway? The documents of the New Testament do not show a consistent pattern. There was flexibility and, therefore, change and adjustment to different needs and circumstances. There is no reason to believe that, when the canon of the New Testament was closed, the Holy Spirit ceased to inspire the Church to adjustments to meet new situations. Ortiz says, 'In the Bible we find the church in only two dimensions.'[7] This is not strictly true even of the New Testament era, for we are already seeing new geographical groupings which may well have been the precursors of the diocesan framework of later episcopacy. Paul, for example, writes to 'the churches of Galatia' and refers elsewhere to 'the people of Macedonia' (Gal. 1:2; 2 Cor. 9:2). What is true of the Church for many centuries is that there were no divisions on doctrinal grounds. We have to wait very largely until the Reformation for that to happen. But the fact remains that in the New Testament we find the embryo of geographical groupings somewhere between the local church and the universal, and the beginnings of episcopacy, which was soon to be established across the entire Christian world. The groupings often seemed to follow political or national boundaries. Thus it could be said that the Church adopted the secular framework. This is not necessarily a bad thing. Jesus sent his people out into the world, and so it was perfectly natural, since they had to work in secular society, that they should have adopted the secular framework of that society. Later the spirit of the world was to penetrate so deeply into the Church that it began more and more disastrously to ape the world's life-style and authoritarian patterns. But that is another story.

But denominations as such were a product of a different age. The Reformation brought about the most serious and damaging divisions in Christendom. The Great Schism between the Eastern and Western Churches was sad enough, but it did reflect the almost totally different worlds that these two large Churches had grown up in. The Schism was really the ultimate recognition of differences that go back to the earliest times. But the Reformation led to a most harmful fragmentation of Christendom. The initial break had at least as many political and economic causes as doctrinal. The most fundamental result was the establishment of national Churches in England, Scotland, Scandinavia, Germany, and Switzerland, which to begin with were quite as tyrannical as, if not more so than, the old united Catholic Church. There were further splits from the national Churches on other issues, such as doctrine and church government. These led to the secession of the Anabaptists, Congregationalists and Methodists in the seventeenth and eighteenth centuries, and the Holiness and Pentecostal Churches in the nineteenth and twentieth centuries.

No one could possibly say that such tearing apart of the Body of Christ was the best that could have happened. Denominations are not God's best plan for his Church. But before this God has shown himself to be willing, according to his grace, to be amazingly accommodating to human weakness.

Thus Moses in the Old Testament allowed divorce 'because of the hardness of their hearts'. It may sometimes be the lesser of two evils. So God has allowed denominations, and blessed them in varying degrees. But his will today is surely that they should be reunited. The Danish philosopher Kierkegaard once wrote about Lutheranism, 'It was meant to be a corrective, but men made it *normative.*' That has been the tragedy of most Churches which have broken away from others, and of most Christian movements. The "corrective" of the Reformation, instead of leading to the correction or reform of the one catholic Church, created instead new Churches, which made the corrections normative and thus became unbalanced themselves and equally in need of reformation.

The charismatic renewal, which is currently one of the strongest movements in the Roman Catholic, Anglican, and Protestant Churches, is faced, as all movements have been in the past, with the dilemma of seeing something more of the eschatological Church than some of the contemporary Church does; of earnestly desiring it; and of being pressured into breaking entirely with the past in order to seize the prize. The temptation to start all over again is sometimes almost overwhelming. But the temptation needs to be resisted. To break with the past and to start building on new foundations has many short-term benefits. But history has proved over and over again that it is like the way 'which seems right to a man, but its end is the way to death' (Prov. 14:12). The past is a graveyard of lost causes, of movements which began with great enthusiasm and the highest ideals, but which ended in death. What is sometimes worse is that they don't die, as the Catholic Apostolic Church has, but linger on interminably, depressing relics of a past moment of rapture. God's way is always to *renew* what he has created. It is not helpful to talk, as some do, about "restoration". This implies that God is putting back what has not been there before. Many renewal movements, in their early days, have thought they were "restoring" something. But when one looks more closely one sees that it has been there all the time, only hidden or inert for the moment. The charismatic movement is not *restoring* the gifts of the Spirit, but there is a *renewal* of them. God has never taken them away; they have just not been claimed, appreciated or fully understood. Nor should we use the word *revolution*. This implies a complete break with the past. God never does that, for he is the God of history as well as the Eternal One; and the Church is so deeply engraved in history that it is impossible to separate the present from the past. But we must not let the past govern the present or obscure the glorious future of the Church. We need to beware of Church perfectionism, of that view which separates the "perfect Church" from the imperfect or apostate. We need to watch when the sabres are rattled and the talk turns ominously to "wineskins". We have heard it all before. Some regard the Lord's return as imminent, and so there is that drive to be part of the specially refined Church which he is coming back for. So said the Catholic Apostolics and the Plymouth Brethren of the nineteenth century, and so have said the Pentecostals and others in the twentieth century. The Lord is coming for a prepared Church, but he is not coming back for a small coterie of charismatics who are too impatient to wait for the rest of the Church. He is preparing the Church for his return. The renewal is well under way; but there is still much to be done.

8

All the Best

My best men are women. General Booth

On the practical level, I suggest that in order to manifest also in the Council itself, and before all men, our faith in the charisms given by the Holy Spirit to all believing Christians...women too should be invited as auditors; unless I am mistaken, they make up half of the human race. Speech of Cardinal Suenens at Vatican II

IT WAS WHEN I saw Margit Sahlin being zipped into her alb at the Engelbrekts Kyrkan in Stockholm that I first began to take seriously the ordination of women. Subsequently on further visits to Denmark and Sweden, I became more and more used to seeing women doing what in some eyes can only be done by men. In 1973 I visited Umea in Northern Sweden for some ecumenical gatherings. There too I found that part of the leadership was taken by a young woman priest called Lisa Tegby. The next time I saw her was in St. Paul's Cathedral at the service to mark the tenth anniversary of the Fountain Trust. We were singing the final hymn and I was standing next to John Trillo, Bishop of Chelmsford, when I spotted Lisa in the congregation. 'Look out,' I said to the bishop, 'there is a Swedish woman priest over there.' After the service was over I introduced Lisa to the bishop. He told her that he was all for women priests, whereupon Lisa planted a kiss on his cheeks! The bishop turned to me and said under his breath, 'Well, that's the first time I've been kissed by a priest!'

In 1975 the General Synod of the Church of England debated the subject of the ordination of women and agreed in principle to it. But the issue has provoked a wide cleavage of opinion amongst the clergy and laity, even with threats of resignation on both sides if women are or are not ordained. It is a difficult subject, and men and women often have strong views on it. It is an emotional issue too, and seems to stir the hearts of people more readily than almost anything else. Some clergy, finding themselves trapped and threatened by women, and emotionally ill-equipped to cope, find their exclusion from ordination a safeguard they are most reluctant to give up. Some women, too, feel threatened by anything remotely like Women's Lib. Safe and snug in their rather restricted feminine role, they dare not adventure out into the competitive world of men, but are perfectly happy to leave 'all that' well alone. It is no good denying that there are strong emotional currents involved which make this subject almost impossible to deal with in a detached manner. Nevertheless, for all that, the various arguments for and against are to be respected and not just dismissed as blind prejudice or emotional bunkum.

So no one today can seriously write a book about ministry without discussing this delicate subject. As I hope to show, it is not a secondary issue. Nor has it been brought nearer to the top of the agenda because of the fuller emancipation which women throughout the world have been able to achieve for themselves. It is an important issue in its own right, which is relevant to our subject of church growth. For if any part of the Church is restricted and hindered from ministry because of the prejudice and false traditions of another part, then the Church will be most fundamentally hindered from growing as it should. So, to put it positively, if it is right for women to be emancipated in the Church as they have been in the world, it will release new growth potential in the Church. But this needs to be established, for there are still many people in our Churches who do not accept the principle of equality between men and women in the Church. We must not judge the opposition's motives, or put it all down to male chauvinism. They certainly claim to have the scriptures and the traditions of the Church on their side, and we need to look carefully at their arguments. But should we be able to show that women should be given equal opportunities to serve alongside men, and that there is nothing in the Church's ministry which should be reserved for men alone, and that this is God's will for his people, then we are likely to see a new and strong growth factor set to work in the Church.

In 1975 Mrs. Margaret Thatcher became the leader of the British Conservative Party. There are some who think that Mrs. Shirley Williams could become the leader of the Labour Party in the years to come. That this should happen in the Conservative Party is amazing; Socialism has always, at least in theory, believed in the equality of the sexes, and Lenin was once reported as saying, 'A revolution without women is unthinkable.' But Mrs. Thatcher is only one of several women who have won their way to top positions in society over the heads of men. One has only to mention Mrs. Golda Meir, former Prime Minister of Israel, and Mrs. Indira Gandhi, the present Prime Minister of India, which is the largest democratic country in the world.

The reaction of some Christians to Mrs. Thatcher's appointment was most illuminating, and shows how deep male prejudice goes. It was to them a sign of moral decadence. Their thinking went something like this. There ought, of course, to be a man at the top. The fact that there is a woman at the head of a political party means that there must be lots of men who are shirking their responsibilities, and not doing their job properly. If a woman has to take authority over men, shame on the men and shame on the nation. In other words, no woman could ever get to the top on merit alone.

It is not surprising that in the Church women should play such a comparatively trivial role. They have been led to believe for centuries that they have nothing very important or serious to contribute, and that there is something weak about the emotional and psychological sides of their nature, which prevents them from taking authority over men, or working alongside men in partnership. And, in any case, many would argue that the Bible has settled the matter for all time, so that no good can ever come from discussing the subject any further.

For centuries women have been subjected to derogatory remarks and belittling attitudes. Like Ophelia in *Hamlet* they have been all too readily dismissed to nunneries or kept firmly in their place, which is the home. They have been treated in the Church as second-class citizens. Epiphanius, a Bishop of Salamis in the fourth century, and an enthusiastic supporter of monasticism, writes against women heretics: 'Courage, servants of God. Let us invest ourselves with all the qualities of men and put to flight this feminine madness.' He goes on to speak disparagingly of women: 'In very truth, women are a feeble race, untrustworthy and of mediocre intelligence.' He had no time for women priests.[1] We may laugh at such ludicrous statements from the fourth century, but the way in which women are treated in the Church today would indicate that similar attitudes are still all too common. It would seem that there are not a few Christian men who do regard women generally as being "of mediocre intelligence". There are still men who would exclude them from the councils of the Church and from any role of leadership in it. Male prejudice against women is still strong in the Church, and it needs to be both recognised and repented of. One has often heard men speak critically of bossy women, as if there was no such thing as a bossy man. Many women have been hurt by an un-Christian attitude and by the sense of rejection which goes with it. Others have been so crushed by male domination that the gifts they have to bring to the Body of Christ have been hidden and unused. In counselling, one has had to deal with cases of women who have been treated as inferior beings either by their husbands or by their ministers and church leaders. So an enormous potential for ministry and growth in the Church has been lost.

There is need for a fresh understanding and appreciation of the dignity of womanhood. This assault on woman, which has been sustained for centuries by the greed and self-indulgence of men, is seen in its most loathsome form in the modern obsession with pornography. For several years one has seen this subject dealt with by Christians almost solely in terms of the harm that is done to *men* by their exposure to pornography. One seldom sees anything said about the effect this has on *women*. One is not only referring to the destructive effects which it has on the minds and souls of those women who are treated as mere sex objects by the pornographers; that in itself is horrifying. But we also have to consider the effects this has on men and their attitudes to women in general, and the results of the large-scale presentation of promiscuity and violence on women, who see themselves thus treated by men as animals to be endlessly exploited. As David Holbrook has written in a letter to *The Times:*[2]

> All pornography is, of its nature, visual rape, and a form of violation to others, which teaches people at large to make use of others for their own satisfaction... Pornography is a form of victimization, and can never be 'normal'. Even the mere titillating nude is a way of robbing another person of something they are felt not to be giving voluntarily. But it is also cruel to triumph over others by making them perform their most creative and intimate acts in public.

A crude but popular rejoinder is that women choose to do this. Yes, but only for considerable financial rewards, and they are often then trapped and helpless, unable to defend themselves from such exploitation, which stems from man's sinful attitude towards womanhood.

R. P. C. Hanson, in an article in *The Times* (March 20th, 1976) has well written:

This flood of pornography represents a ruthless and disgusting exploitation of woman. It is a strange fact that the women's liberation movement appears not to have noticed this. While our generation prides itself on having made great progress in emancipating women, at the same time our pornographic industry exploits them as never before. How many voyeuses are there? This is an industry run for the benefit of the lustful male, and depending upon the exploitation of women, but no strenuous champions of female liberty condemn it. While we proclaim the equality of women with one voice, we declare them a million times over as mere sex objects, mere occasions for arousing male desire, with another. Every time an almost or wholly naked 'model' is photographed in the daily papers, every time a similar figure is used to advertise cars or petrol or cigarettes, the same blatant exploitation is practised. Yet nobody seems to think it is wrong.

We see this prejudice against women in all kinds of areas. The psychologist Freud regarded woman as a deficient human being, and there are still those who regard most women as sub-clinically neurotic. In contrast to Freud's mainly negative account of feminine psychology and personality, based on the woman's frustration at being a woman and her desire to be a man, Ann Ulanov sees both male and female as constituting a complete humanity: 'The feminine is half of human wholeness, an essential part of it... Masculine and feminine elements exist only in relation to each other and complement rather than fight each other!' We see this in greater detail when we come to look at the kind of complementary roles that men and women can have in partnership in the Church. Over the centuries women have been forced to retreat into the one role they alone can fulfil — motherhood. Almost the only other option for them was prostitution, as something they could call their own. But both in the home and on the streets women were kept by men, and exploited for their pleasure. This was tolerable when women were mostly married. At least they were protected from some of the more sordid sides of life. But when many women found themselves committed to the single life, their protected lives became for them prisons from which they longed to break free. One can begin to understand the fury of the suffragette movement, for many women at the start of the twentieth century had nothing worth living for. Of course, the picture is not all black. There were women who found fulfilment and happiness. But the overall picture is a bad one, for which men were mostly to blame. Many of these wrong attitudes have been challenged and changed in our day. But the Church has been slower than the rest of society at attaining to the new and healthier attitudes towards women. It is sad when we see the Church lagging behind the world, apparently impervious to what the Holy Spirit is saying and doing!

This issue is not only of importance in itself; it also challenges the Church to think more clearly about the ministry in general, and exactly what ordination is, and what constitutes leadership. For if the Church's understanding of the ministry of men is hazy, then ordaining women will only add to the confusion. It would seem, in fact, that a clearer and more biblical understanding of ministry would make it easier for most to see the rightness of ordaining women. But if we think in terms of the one-man ministry, then a one-woman ministry would be equally unsatisfactory. On the other hand if we accept the biblical principle of plurality of leadership in the Church, it is easier for people to accept women in partnership with men in church leadership. It was, for instance, easier for the Lutheran Church in Sweden to accept in principle the ordination of women because at the time (1960) the Church had a good many team ministries, especially in the country districts. The issue at stake today is not only that of ordination of women, but also of our whole understanding of ministry itself. The controversy over the ordination of women is forcing the Church to reconsider what ministry is all about.

But it is important for another reason. It is not only the

question of whether women may share with men the leadership of the Church which is at stake, but also the whole matter of the relationship between men and women and their distinctive roles in the home and society. The Christian Church of all societies ought to be an example to the rest of the world of healthy and mutually fulfilling relationships between men and women. Men and women should not be seen as competitors, or as contestants in the battle of the sexes, but as partners in the ministry of the Church, with different roles as we shall see, but complementing each other. Each should be supportive of the other. Men should be able to draw out women's contribution, and encourage them to share it with the whole body. Women should equally encourage men to develop their roles. Both should have a mutually submissive attitude to each other, listening to each other, learning from each other. Men especially need to be patient as women adjust slowly to their new roles and opportunities.

But it is also important that the ecumenical aspects are not forgotten. One of the arguments employed against the ordination of women in the Church of England was that it would make ecumenical relations difficult with some other churches. Obviously relations with the Free Churches, most of whom ordain women, would, if anything, improve. But the Roman Catholic Church and the Eastern Orthodox Churches are still opposed to the ordination of women, and it might, so some have argued, hinder future relations if the Church of England were to go ahead and ordain women. So many changes have already taken place in recent years that it is difficult to predict what will happen in the Roman Catholic Church in the coming years. But there is a growing consensus which favours ordination of women to the priesthood. On balance it is perhaps better that Anglicans and others, if they feel that the Holy Spirit is guiding them in this direction, should go ahead with it. We need not wait for every initiative to come from Rome. In fact, waiting for Rome's decision might well prove counter-productive in the long run.

Although the General Synod of the Church of England at its summer meeting in 1975 decided in principle to ordain women, it also decided not to do so immediately. This seems to have been a wise decision for a number of reasons which will be discussed later in this chapter.

The biblical evidence and its interpretation

In 1958 when the question of the ordination of women was being debated in Sweden, the main argument which eventually carried the day was that women had been excluded from ordination because of the attitude to them which prevailed in the first century, which was reflected in the New Testament, and particularly in the attitude of Paul. But now, so the argument went, these attitudes have changed; we are now free to ordain women. There were, of course, other arguments for and against. But this was the main one, which was powerfully backed by the State itself, impatient to bring the Church in line with the new and popular attitudes towards the equality of the sexes which then prevailed in Sweden. But it is not a good enough argument, in my view, upon which to base one's case. The case for accepting women in full partnership with men in Christian leadership rests on far more substantial reasoning.

We need to turn first to Genesis. In chapter 1 the creation of man in the image of God is said to be "male and female" without any suggestion of subordination of the female to the male (v. 27). God's command to them to 'be fruitful and multiply, and fill the earth and subdue it' (v. 28) is directed to both male and female in partnership. There is no suggestion of the female having a subordinate role. In chapter 2, the story of woman's creation from the rib of man, there is no suggestion that woman is in any way inferior or need be submissive to the man. She was to be his helper, in other words to work with him in partnership to till and keep the garden into which God had brought them. Only after the Fall in chapter 3 is the note of subordination struck, and we are surely no more to take the words 'and he shall rule over you'

(v. 16) as the unchanging will of God, than we are to take all the other curses in this chapter. For surely Jesus Christ came to remove them. He came as the second Adam to do what the first Adam failed to do. In any case, the subordination mentioned in Genesis 3 has to do with the relationship of husband and wife to each other, and need not necessarily be stretched to include the relationship between men and women in the Church at large.

Now it is true that Paul quotes the creation narrative in 1 Corinthians 11 in his arguments about the subordination of the wife to the husband. It is important to realise that Paul is mainly concerned with the marriage relationship, not with the larger issue of the role of women in society. In his day that role was so small as to be insignificant. In 1 Corinthians 11:11-12 Paul makes a most interesting statement. 'Nevertheless in the Lord woman is not independent of man *nor man of woman*: for as woman was made from man, so man is now born of woman. And all things are from God.' Here, after discussing the husband-wife relationship and asserting that woman came from man, and was created for man, he states the new general principle that men and women are to be partners together. There are not a few who frankly disagree with Paul's interpretation of Genesis in this passage. But what we need to remember is that Paul is writing a *corrective* letter to the Corinthians on a whole range of issues. We need to exercise similar care, for example, when we examine 1 Corinthians 12 and 14, if we are not to distort Paul's understanding of spiritual gifts. He was writing mainly to correct abuses and to encourage the proper use of gifts. We have to bear this in mind when interpreting what Paul is saying about the proper use of these gifts.

Similarly Paul is concerned about the way in which women were usurping authority, and using their new-found emancipation to disrupt the Church. His teaching, therefore, is to correct this abuse. Remember what Kierkegaard said about Luther. He was a corrective — but men made his teaching normative. The same thing can equally be said about Paul's teaching in 1 Corinthians and 1 Timothy. Paul meant these passages to be correctives, but men have made them normative, and interpreted them so as to keep women in a place of subordination in the Church.

Whilst we are looking at Paul we need to examine the other two passages which are usually quoted in support of the view that Paul wanted to keep women in submission to men. 1 Corinthians 14:34-6, like the other passage in 1 Corinthians, can be interpreted in terms of husband-wife relations rather than the role of women in the Church. The word *gunaikes* can be translated "wives" as well as "women". In any case, in 1 Corinthians 11 Paul does allow women both to pray and prophesy in church. Here he probably has in mind wives asking their husbands questions during the service. It is likely that men and women sat separately, and so this would have caused quite a disturbance. On this passage William Barclay comments, 'It would certainly be very wrong to take these words of Paul out of the context for which they were written.' And Leon Morris in his commentary writes, 'We must exercise due caution in applying his principle to our own very different situation.'[4] There are also some textual problems about this passage, and some scholars believe it to have been an interpolation. The word translated "to speak" literally means to "chat", which would suggest that Paul does not have preaching, praying or prophesying in mind.

The third passage is 1 Timothy 2:11-15. The context again suggests the home rather than the church. The authority mentioned is related to teaching, not necessarily to leadership in the church. What the passage seems to be indicating is a prohibition of women teaching men with authority in the sense that they establish the norms of doctrine. As we shall be seeing, this is definitely not the role in which women normally excel. This may be the reason why Paul goes on to remind Timothy that it was Eve, not Adam, who was deceived by Satan.

Paul's concern in all these passages is *behavioural* rather than *doctrinal*. As William Barclay says, 'In all likelihood what was uppermost in his mind was the lax state of Corinth and the feeling that nothing, absolutely nothing, must be done which would bring upon the infant Church the faintest suspicion of immodesty.' Those who wish on the grounds of scripture to prohibit female leadership in the Church need to produce much more evidence than these three passages if they are going to convince others.

What is much more important is to see Paul's teaching in Galatians, where he argues positively for freedom, 'There is neither Jew nor Greek, there is neither slave nor free, *there is neither male nor female*; for you are all one in Christ Jesus' (3:28). Sometimes the apostles said things which were beyond themselves. Peter did this in the house of Cornelius, when in spite of the deep prejudice he had against Gentiles, he opened the Kingdom of Heaven to them, and baptised them into the Christian Church without first asking them to become Jews. So Paul, who does at times seem to have a prejudice against women, declares their charter of liberty: 'There is neither male nor female.' No one would seriously dispute, except in countries like South Africa, that there should be any racial or social barriers in the Christian Church or that people should be debarred from leadership on grounds of colour or social prestige alone. There is the strongest possible implication in this classic statement of Paul's that he meant the principle of equality to apply to the position of women in the Church as it did to racial and social equality. The fact that it has taken so long to come to this understanding is not so strange when one considers how deep has been the prejudice against women and how established have been sexual taboos in world-wide society. But that we may have come near to the point of break-through is exhilarating. For Jesus Christ came to restore what had been lost by the first Adam, and to take people back to God's original purposes, of partnership in his creation.

The divisions in Jewish society in Jesus's day could be seen in stark relief in the temple itself. There were parts of the temple from which all Gentiles were excluded. Other parts were out-of-bounds to women. Then, of course, there were those sacred parts into which only members of the priestly caste could enter, and the holy of holies from which all were excluded except the high priest, who could only enter once a year. We see how revolutionary the Epistle to the Galatians is in relationship to the temple in Jerusalem. God has broken down the middle wall of partition in order to create a new society of those who recognise no racial, social or sexual barriers to fellowship. But the power of prejudice is strong. It took centuries to overthrow slavery in the old Roman Empire. We still have our racial and social apartheids. But the emancipation of women has taken longest, and the struggle for their liberation in the Church has still a long way to go before their freedom can be assured. The ministry needs liberation today from its many traditional shackles, and one of these is the way in which women have been held down and prevented from fulfilling their ministries.

When we come to consider Jesus's own attitude to women, we need to remember the position that women held in society in his day. The wives of Greek citizens were confined to separate quarters and were little more than the property of their husbands. Plato disagreed with the attitudes of his day and pleaded for the equality of the sexes, but Aristotle regarded women as naturally inferior. According to Roman law wives were under the complete control of their husbands. They were not allowed to own property, but they held a position of great importance in the normal home, which was authoritarian in structure. In Judaism the famous passage in Proverbs 31:10f. shows that a wife had an honourable role, and a fair degree of freedom. She could buy land and be involved in farming. She could also buy and sell in the market. Women played an important part in national life, too. Esther was one of the saviours of the Jewish nation; Deborah's exploits are described in Judges and she was one of the judges herself. It was, however, as in other matters, the rabbinical additions to the law which reveal how anti-feminine Jewish society had become in the days of our Lord.

J. Jeremias brings this out in his book *Jerusalem in the Time of Jesus*.[6] Where the rabbinical rules were observed, women took no part whatever in public life, Jeremias tells us, and were so thoroughly concealed by their clothes that a man did not recognise his own mother.[7] There was a rabbinical aphorism of this time, 'It is better to burn the Torah than to teach it to women', which shows how deeply distrustful the Rabbis were of women. Women also had an inferior status because they could not enter into the covenant relationship through circumcision. The worship too was primarily the responsibility and activity of men. Women had to keep silence in the synagogue. Thus many Jewish men prayed, 'Blessed be God who has not made me a heathen, a slave or a woman.' One finds similar attitudes in Hinduism and amongst Moslems. In India and Arab countries the position of women is similar to that which Jesus encountered in his day.

We should be careful not to exaggerate the political and social disadvantages of women in the world of the first century. Nevertheless, they were definitely regarded universally as of inferior status to men. But Christianity changed all this. As Michael Green writes, 'The opportunity of finding a faith where they could be given an equality of status and a real sphere of service must have helped many women to put their trust in Jesus as Lord.'[8] If that is true, then it is worth pondering how many women are prevented from taking the gospel seriously today because they see the prejudices that Christians have; they are inhibited from becoming involved in the Church because they are unprepared to leave the society of the world, where they are accepted and protected by the law so far as discrimination is concerned, and to join another society which continues to practise discrimination. Michael Green, in the same passage, points out that women played a leading part in the spread of the gospel in the early years of the Church.

But Jesus's attitude to women was revolutionary in his day. His coming, in the first place, was due to the faithfulness of the Virgin Mary. She co-operated simply and truly with the work of the Holy Spirit in her. And we notice the Spirit-inspired ministry of Anna, the prophetess, and of Elizabeth, which stands out starkly in contrast to the disobedience of her husband Zechariah. When Jesus began his public ministry there was apparently a group of women who travelled with him and the other disciples to care for them (see Luke 8:1-3 and Mark 15:40-1).

When it comes to Jesus's death and resurrection we see again the faithful way in which the women cared for him. They were the first witnesses of his resurrection, and it was they who brought the news first to the rest of the Church. When we consider that it was regarded as indecent for a Jewish man to have a conversation with a woman in public, we can appreciate how scandalised society was when Jesus not only did this — but also conversed with Samaritan and Gentile women, even with women of the streets! There was one woman who was ritually unclean and was actually breaking the law by being in the crowd and touching Jesus, yet he healed her (Mark 5:25-34). So one could go on. Jesus's attitude to women was the very opposite of that of most of his contemporaries, Jew or Gentile. We may not deduce from this that he necessarily approved of a future Church having women in positions of leadership. To have gone the whole way towards emancipating women then would have been impossible. Society would not have stood for it. But neither can we argue that, because he only appointed male apostles, he intended all future ministers to be male. On this issue, as on that of slavery, Jesus was silent. But the way in which he behaved and acted would lead one to believe that he would approve of men and women as partners in leadership and ministry, and that this was his real intention for his Church.

Certainly when we come to the Acts and the Epistles we see a freedom which was in marked contrast to the attitudes and taboos of that time. Entry to the New Covenant was by baptism, in which men and women both shared. Women, therefore, attained fundamental equality with men. There was 'neither male nor female' in the Christian Church. In

Romans 16:1-3, a woman called Phoebe is called by Paul "our sister" and a deacon. (There is a common gender for deacon and deaconess in Greek.) She is highly commended by Paul to the Church. Some women are called "fellow-workers" by Paul in his letters. It was Priscilla, together with Aquila, her husband, who shared in instructing the great preacher Apollos (Acts 18:26). Philip, the evangelist, had four unmarried daughters who prophesied (Acts 21:9), and Acts 2:18 and 1 Corinthians 11:5 assume that women will prophesy in Church. We see in these references a freedom given to women to minister with (and presumably to) men which was unprecedented for those days.

But gradually tradition and prejudice reasserted themselves, and women were put back in their place of subordination. It was the rise of monasticism which was to give women the opportunities for full-time ministry which were barred to them in the normal life of the Church. Many took their chance and left their mark on the larger Church as a result. There is an amusing story which, if true, illustrates how deeply prejudiced even the most saintly were in this matter. Bernard of Clairvaux was once kneeling before a statue of the Virgin. Apparently, when she opened her lips to speak, he said to her, 'Silence, it is not permitted to a woman to speak in the church.' It is depressing to dwell on how much the Church down the centuries has been impoverished because women have not had their say.

Through the period of the Church Fathers, the medieval Church and the Reformation, there is a general agreement, and the role of women in the Church (as also in the world) was of an inferior and generally subordinate nature. This has been taken even further in the Orthodox Church, where it is a commonly observed custom that women do not approach the sacrament during menstruation and only after the menopause may a woman enter the sanctuary. It is interesting, on the other hand, to find a far more liberal attitude amongst revivalists and the more extreme sects. This is reflected, for example, in groups like the Anabaptists, who were so viciously persecuted by the Reformers, and yet were ahead of their times in so many respects. They saw things too early and paid a heavy price for their spiritual insight. George Fox was another prophet who, like the Anabaptists, recognised the ministry of women in the Churches. William Booth, founder of the Salvation Army, allowed women to have an equal role with men from the beginning of his movement. His rule, first formulated in 1870, contained a clause stating that 'Women shall be employed as preachers, itinerants or otherwise and class leaders and as such shall have appointments given to them in the preachers' plan and they shall be eligible for any office and to speak and vote at all official meetings.' Women were to have an equal share with men, and to hold any position of authority or power in the Army. According to Flora Larsson, 'A woman is not to be kept back from any position of power or influence merely on account of her sex.'[11] William Booth's wife Catherine on one occasion stood up in a service and said, 'I want to say a word.' William responded with the famous words, 'My dear wife wishes to speak... Tonight my wife will be the preacher': a revolutionary act in Victorian England. She became a famous and effective preacher.[12] But their daughter Kate proved by the age of seventeen to be such a magnetic preacher that when rowdies threatened to drown a meeting Booth would order, 'Put on Kate, she's our last card.' Evangeline Booth was an accomplished orator, and rose to become the first woman General of the Salvation Army. The Pentecostal Movement has also produced some outstanding women leaders, including Aimee Semple McPherson, who drew huge crowds for many years to the Angelus Temple which she founded in Los Angeles; Kathryn Kuhlman, who attracted capacity audiences every month in the huge Shrine Auditorium in Los Angeles; and Jean Darnall, who ministered at the Angelus Temple before coming to Britain in 1968.

One of the keys to resolving the apparent contradiction in Paul's writings, in which he seems to encourage the role of women in partnership with men in some passages, whereas in others he wants them to accept a definitely subordinate position, is to distinguish between the Church and marriage. We have already seen that any society, from the heights of the glorious Trinity to the smallest gathering of people, needs leadership, and that leadership should normally be plural not singular. We have also seen that when you have a team leadership there is normally a need for a chairman or president. Now this is true for a local church. Each such local church should have a number of elders or leaders, and there is usually amongst them a natural chairman. So the same principle should hold true for marriage and the home. Every new marriage is a new society formed. There is a need for leadership. Since leadership should be plural, it is shared by husband and wife, who mutually submit to one another. It is important to notice that the words of Paul — 'Be subject to one another out of reverence for Christ' — come before the specific injunction to wives — 'Let wives also be subject in everything to their husbands' (Eph. 5:21, 24). When children are born they submit to their parents, until they are adult enough to share the leadership of the home with them. But, as in every other society, there needs to be a head, and in the case of marriage this is always to be the husband as a divine ordinance. This does not mean that the husband bosses the wife around, or that the wife is simply her husband's slave. We have already seen how the new Christian concept of marital relationships was anathema to the commonly accepted views of society in the Graeco-Roman world of the first century. It means that husband and wife share the leadership of the home together, but the husband is the chairman or president, so to speak.

Now we need to keep these two "societies" separate in our thinking if we are to understand the New Testament properly. Thus women are to keep silence in the church in relationship to their husbands, but may freely speak, lead and contribute in relationship to the church. There seems no reason why women should not be elders in the church, where the principle of plurality is followed, mutually submitting to their fellow elders. But wives, when they are in the home, need to be subject in everything to their husbands. It is possible (and sometimes happens today), that a woman may be an elder in a church, and, therefore, the rest of the church submits to her, together with the other elders. But when she is in her home, she submits to her husband as head, even though he may not be a fellow elder in the church of which they are both members. The relationship between the church society and the intertwined marital one is a delicate subject, but it is important to make this distinction if we are to make any sense of what Paul and others are saying about this matter in the New Testament. Those passages which are most frequently quoted in defence of all-male leadership (1 Cor. 11:3-16; 14:33-6; 1 Tim. 2:11-15) need to be understood in the light of this distinction between the Church community and the home. In the New Testament it is often hard to make this distinction, as the Church was often in the home, and the Church was communitarian in a sense in which it seldom is today. But if this distinction is maintained, then the Pauline passages do not appear to contradict the main tenor of the New Testament teaching on this subject.

But it is when we turn to Christ himself that we find most help. We have seen that the pattern of all ministry is Jesus Christ. He is our greatest example, and was constantly encouraging his disciples to follow him and be like him. But there is much more to it than that. Our ministry is not only to be patterned on his, but it is also to draw its inspiration and very essence from him, for we are in him and he is in us. 'I will not leave you desolate,' Jesus said. 'I will come to you... In that day you will know that I am in my Father, and you in me, and I in you' (John 14:18, 20). It is impossible to think of ministry at all without the living Christ of today, who by the Holy Spirit dwells incarnationally in us. *But what sex is the ascended Christ?* It is an important question, because John tells us that 'When he appears we shall be like him, for we shall see Him as he is' (1 John 3:2). It is important also because the ministry gifts of Ephesians 4 are the gifts of the *ascended*

Christ (Eph. 4:7-11). Now the Lord Jesus Christ is ascended in his perfect humanity *rather than his masculinity*. It is the incarnate Jesus who is male rather than the ascended Christ. Both the Te Deum and the Athanasian Creed assert this. In the former, the words 'When thou tookest upon thee to deliver man' should read 'thee man to deliver', and the Latin word *homo*, not *vir*, is used. The Athanasian Creed also, in speaking of "manhood" taken into God uses the word *humanitas* (humanity).[13] If, therefore, the pattern of our ministry is to be related to the ascended Christ, and not to be simply a matter of following the example of the incarnate Christ of the first century, then there should be "neither male nor female" when it comes to ministry in the Church.

We need now to turn to the important question of the differing roles of men and women in ministry in the Church. When we say, 'There is neither male nor female', we are not asserting that there is no difference (apart from the physical) between men and women. This was the view of some of the early Gnostics, and is an added reason for Paul's correctives to the Corinthians and to Timothy. There were those within the early churches who were pressing for a sexual revolution in their day not unlike the Women's Lib of our own. There were then as now feminists who refused to accept their femininity in any other area than the physical, and in so doing they were denigrating the work of God in creation, and causing great damage in the Church. I have tried to avoid as much as possible the use of the word "equality", since it can be more confusing than useful. I have preferred to use the term "partnership". Men and women should be equal partners in the ministry and leadership of the Church. But the word "equality" as used today tends to imply a kind of uniformity, which is an inaccurate description of male/female partnership. In that partnership men and women will normally fulfil different roles in mutual submission to one another. John MacQuarrie has written about this, 'Egalitarianism in its more naïve forms conceals many fallacies and often militates against true human worth.'[14]

There is no need to spend time on the obvious hormonal differences between men and women and their different roles in intercourse and reproduction. But sexuality is an intrinsic part of the psychology and personality of every human being, and this involves our emotions, our minds and our wills. This has nothing to do with superiority and inferiority. What, however, it has to do with is the different role that men and women will have in the Body of Christ. John MacQuarrie reminds us that the masculine mind tends to be 'analytical, critical, specialised, discursive; the feminine, by contrast, is aiming at completeness and is intuitive'.[15] Erik Erikson has observed, for example, that girls will use building blocks to construct interiors or enclosures in which there is peace and security. Boys, on the other hand, construct exterior scenes, towers, and the like. He sees this as reflecting the structure of their own bodies. But instead of giving this a Freudian interpretation, Erikson gives the woman's role a positive valuation as expressing a 'productive inner-bodily space' thus complementing the outgoing male drive.[16] Another psychologist, R. S. Lee, is quoted by John MacQuarrie as showing the difference between boys and girls in their attitudes to morality. Boys see morality in terms of rules and moral principles, girls in terms of ideals.[17] In his article on 'God and the feminine', John MacQuarrie goes on to the important insight of C. J. Jung that the masculine and feminine types of personality are not found in isolation, the masculine in men and the feminine in women, 'but that every human being, whether man or woman, has both masculine and feminine elements in his or her personality'. This new understanding of man makes it impossible for us to absolutise on male and female roles, other than the obvious physical ones. Again it should be a matter of complementariness or partnership. Adam was an incomplete being until the creation of Eve.

When we see this and begin to apply it to the concepts of ministry in Ephesians 4, some interesting factors can be noticed. There are some of these spheres of ministry which are particularly suitable for men. Apostolic ministry in both its travelling aspect and its teaching and leadership roles is more suited to males, whereas pastoral ministry, which includes understanding how people tick, and requires sympathy and intuitive skills, is more suited to women. The teaching ministry, which requires a more analytical approach, is more suited to men, while women have more the kind of mind which is open to prophetic gifts. Both men and women in their different ways can be accomplished in evangelism. But here too there is a need for partnership, for there are some people who may be resistant to a male approach, while at the same time responsive to a female line. Women have made very effective evangelists, and sometimes have been able to get through to people who have remained impervious to a male approach. For instance, when my wife and I visited India in 1975 we found that my wife had much wider scope for her ministry than I had for mine. This was, in part, due to the fact that whereas men and women tended to come to her for help and counsel, only the men came to me. Obviously the Priscilla-Aquila partnership was most effective in the early Church. God created male and female "in his own image", and if this is so, then the image of God needs both men and women in partnership to reflect it faithfully.

It is interesting that children are conditioned by their very toys. Boys are "thing-orientated" and generally play with bricks and mechanical toys, whereas girls are "people-orientated" and play with dolls. Their roles in adult life tend to remain the same, and when we examine churches today we find similar factors. Most church leadership is male dominated, and tends to devalue the personal aspects of ministry. Many churches seem to concentrate on either intellectual or materialistic considerations. The ministers are still playing with their bricks. When female leadership predominates, personal ministry and the social life of the Church tend to be emphasised. The dolls are out again.

But even in mental abilities men and women differ. In an article in *The Times,* Dr. Jeffrey Gray has shown the difference between men and women in the pattern of such abilities.

'Women score more highly on tests of verbal I.Q. than do men, and men score more highly on tests of visuo-spatial I.Q.'[18] This would seem to account, too, for the successes that women tend to have over men in the popular TV programme *Mastermind*.

It seems that in this whole matter we have to steer a careful course between those who want to abolish all sexual distinctiveness, and those who want to define the roles of men and women in an absolute sense. Dr. Sherwin Bailey has written well about this:[19]

> In Christ...sex is neither abolished nor transcended but sexual division and antagonism are done away, and with them traditional notions of headship and subjection, of superiority and inferiority. Instead there comes into being a new creation which is yet the realisation of God's original purpose... The structure of sexual relationship, as ordained by God, can only be discovered in the way He has willed — that is in and through the relation itself... as man and woman live and work together in responsible partnership.

In 1975 the General Synod of the Church of England agreed in principle to ordain women to the priesthood. But it also agreed that the time was not ripe to do so yet. This was probably a wise, though for women an exasperating, decision. The ecumenical factor should not itself determine the issue. Dr. James Packer regards such ordination as "decidedly inexpedient" and gives several good reasons for this.[20] They range from the ecumenical one we have already mentioned to problems arising from possessing the legal freehold of a parish. One reason, of course, is that we are not particularly short of clergy at the present time. Another is that many sections of the Church are against such a step and this would be 'unfair and wounding to first women presbyters'. Certainly, in Sweden women experienced much suffering in the early years when they were first ordained. No doubt, there are women prepared for this suffering. But it is not something one should go ahead with lightly. However, the most important reason that Dr. Packer gives is that the ordaining of women 'would distract from the clericalist malaise of Christian Ministry today, when our first task should be to recognise the disease and attempt its cure'. He quotes a shrewd comment of Alan Richardson's'[21]

> The question which should now be asked concerns the ministry of the Church as a whole, not merely the question of the admission of women to the orders of ministry... A much more radical reformation of the Church's ministry is urgently needed... The focusing of attention upon the question of the admission of women to the priesthood diverts energies which ought today to be directed towards the more urgently needed correction of the prevailing one-sided view of the nature and task of the Church's ministry. The demand for the ordination of women to the priesthood is largely based upon this erroneous view... It arises from the false assumption that the only way in which a woman (or a man, for that matter) can participate in the *real* ministry of the Church is to join the professionals by acquiring priest's orders... To admit women to the priest-hood would leave the present unsatisfactory situation exactly where it is and would do nothing to reform what is wrong... It would do nothing to promote the development of a wide variety of ministries, which is the Church's most immediate need.[21]

Alan Richardson hits the nail on the head. If our present attitudes to ministry are wrong, and if the ministry itself urgently needs this reformation, then to ordain women to that same ministry with all its aberrations will simply make matters worse.

There does seem, however, to be a simple solution, which follows the main arguments of this book. If every local church should have a plurality of leadership, there seems no reason why women should not share with men in such group leadership, provided, of course, they are called and equipped for this. They do not need to be ordained to do this. This is a possibility which Dr. Packer allows for: 'membership of a group presbyterate', he calls it.[22] Although such women would not have the *status* and the Church's recognition of leadership, they could *function* in the same way as men. They would not be able to celebrate the Holy Communion, but again we have seen that this is not so important a function as some would assert. The service is important, but who takes it is of secondary value. Indeed the New Testament does not ever tell us who does, and it does not seem to have been an important issue in those times.

If we see things in this light, then the practical issues can take care of themselves. Some have said that a married woman would be torn in her loyalties between her home and the Church. But is not a married man torn in a not wholly dissimilar way? Does not a child need a father as well as a mother? If we see ministry and leadership in terms of team work and partnership there seems no reason why a woman should not be supported during the period of her pregnancy and later confinement by the other elders until she is more free to give time to her role as a church leader. Admittedly a one-woman ministry would be unhealthy, but no more so than a one-man ministry.

In 1968 the Lambeth Conference said that 'the New Testament does not encourage Christians to think that nothing should be done for the first time'. The Holy Spirit is leading the Church today in new and exciting ways, not least in the discovery that since in Christ "there is neither male nor female", men and women can discover a new and glorious partnership in ministry, which means that they can both fulfil their different roles in harmony and complementariness.

9

No Other Option

To have opted for love: that choice opens in a man a wound from which he never recovers. Prior of Taizé, *Struggle and Contemplation,* p. 28

WE HAVE NO option but to love one another. It was the only new commandment that Jesus gave us. It is all we have to do, but how difficult to do it! We cannot opt for love and at the same time escape the inevitable wounds which we sustain and which we inflict on others. To love and to be loved is to be vulnerable and open-ended. It means to be close enough for others to hurt us, and it is the fear of being hurt which more often than not holds us back from coming too close to others. 'This is my commandment,' Jesus said, 'that you love one another as I have loved you' (John 15:12).

We might have chosen another word for this chapter — *commitment.* It is being used frequently to describe a new concept of relationship between Christians. But it is a harsh-sounding word. There is something about it which makes it unsuitable as a description of Christian relationships. A husband and wife commit themselves to one another, but "commitment" is an inadequate word to describe the new relationship which has come about. Nevertheless, it is understandable why some are using the term more frequently today. The word "love" has been so sentimentalised and robbed of its true meaning that many are reluctant to use it to describe the new human relationship which exists between Christians, which is different from any other kind of relationship. *Christian love means a mutual commitment of people to one another*, and this aspect needs to be stressed at the present time. Cardinal Mercier of Belgium, one of the great ecumenical pioneers, once said, 'In order to be united with one another we must love one another; in order to love one another we must know one another; in order to know one another we must come out and meet one another.' He was too tactful a man to have added, 'and in the final analysis we must commit ourselves to one another'. If that is the rightful goal of all true ecumenical endeavours, then it is also the true basis of all realistic Christian fellowship. We cannot at the end of the day say we really love one another, if we are not prepared to be committed to one another, with all that this entails of care, submission and authority.

Someone has defined cancer as "exuberant growth without order". If we are going to discover and experience some of the secrets of dynamic and spontaneous growth, then we ought also to recognise the need for order and discipline in the Church. William Barclay has put it well when he writes, 'Community means discipline, and discipline means authority. Whenever any group of people agree to come together, whether it is in a Church or in a golf club, there have to be rules by which they live. That is, there must be discipline.'[1] Just as the human body needs a skeleton, so every Church needs a structure. But it is here that we are confronted with dangers. The very word "authority" and its Greek equivalent (*exousia*), as we shall see, conjure up thoughts of harshness and totalitarianism. That is why we have deliberately stressed the word "love". We need to see everything we mean by "commitment" in terms of love, and not to talk about commitment and throw in "love" to sweeten the pill. It is inconceivable to think of love, if it is anything like the divine pattern, in any other terms than that of a real and free commitment of people to one another.

One does not need to look far in the New Testament to see this principle. In fact we see it everywhere. It is part of the very essence of the Church. The analogy of the human body, which is Paul's favourite way of describing the Church, implies a commitment, or it ceases to be a body at all. But at the same time, the quality of love is there also. Thus Paul sees Christian growth in terms of 'speaking the truth in love' and "bodily growth" as needing to be "in love" (Eph. 4:15-16). In 1 Corinthians 12, Paul sees the Church as possessing a nervous system like the human body so that 'members may have the same care for one another. If one member suffers, all suffer together; if one member is honoured, all rejoice together' (vv. 25-6). If the Church is to grow, it needs to have the kind of sympathy and understanding which is expressed in these passages. Growth is often a painful process. It is not all joy by any means. Only growth "in love" will succeed in holding the body together and preventing the kind of destructive division which is contrary to the Spirit of Christ.

All this is particularly important because of the kind of society most of us live in, which seems to have lost altogether the capacity to be a community. Typical of this is the blurb on the cover of The Infernal Grove, volume 2 of Malcolm Muggeridge's autobiography The Chronicle of Wasted Time. 'Johnson needed Boswell, but Malcolm Muggeridge needs no one else.' This is how modern man views life today, and the whole emphasis of society is so to organise life that you need no one else. So we have the deep loneliness of modern man, with all the psychological disorders associated with it, and the anonymity of life with all its frustrations and dullness. Another example of this can be seen in the development of the dance over the past centuries. The community-style barn dancing and the "Gay Gordons" type of dance were once popular, when you mixed your partners and shared your own life with the whole community. Then there was ballroom dancing, when you picked your own partners and stayed with them — just two people in a world of their own. But the modern dance does not even encourage partners. You are virtully dancing on your own. Like modern society you have been atomised into loneliness and often despair, too. So man has broken up the old small communities, which contributed security and care to large numbers of people. They were small enough to cater for everyone, and numerous enough to cover a wide area. But with the coming of the large industrial cities it became infinitely harder for the communal aspects of living to be effective. Even then, the old slum streets were, to some extent, communities. The new modern cities, with their tower blocks and their modern attitudes to life and their spirit of independence have almost completely lost any sense of community, and do not particularly want to rediscover it. The old extended families of pre-Victorian days have become our modern hermetically sealed nuclear families, breeding-grounds for delinquent rebels and potential criminals. In the Bible the responsibility for social care was laid fairly and squarely on the family, "extended" as it was. Today the State is supposed to do the caring. David Sheppard writes about this:[2]

> In much of our society, with its emphasis on individuals standing on their own feet, the man would have been expected to sort out his own problems. In the Bible, as in rural countries today, orphans and old people would not be a charge on the community at large, because the extended family came to the rescue.

He goes on to show how in the big city of today the extended family has disappeared. This may be an exaggeration — but the evidence points clearly to a marked change in social patterns in urban areas, and the swift erosion of the old extended family structure.

But in many ways the Church is not much better off. In the United States some years ago, when "drive-in" theatres and banks were a novelty, someone built a "drive-in church" and advertised it accordingly: 'Worship in the privacy of your own automobile.' We may laugh at such naivety, if it were not too close for comfort to many of our churches. All you need to do is to substitute "pew" for "automobile" and you have a description of the modern church. What a terrible distortion of the Church the New Testament is talking about! If the Church of the West is approaching a time of persecution, then there needs to be a completely new attitude and commitment to one another if it is to survive. Richard Wurmbrand tells the story in one of his books of the hideous happenings in the notorious Black Room in a Bucharest prison. It was a windowless underground chamber with water dripping from the roof which kept the floor awash, and even in summer it was bitterly cold. On one occasion eighteen middle-aged or elderly members of the National Peasant party were thrust into it. Wurmbrand tells us:[3]

> To avoid freezing to death they formed themselves into a human snake in the darkness. Each man clung to the one in front for warmth as they stamped around in an endless circle, splashed from head to foot in filth. Often a man collapsed, but the others always dragged him up from the water and forced him on.

Thus they survived because they were committed in love to one another. The Church can only survive in times of persecution and hardship when all the members are committed to each other. Those who do not join the human chain of life will perish. *There are no other options* open to us.

If we look at Ephesians 4 we see the need for this commitment expressed in the metaphor of the body which Paul is so fond of. He writes of the Church becoming more and more like Christ, 'from whom the whole body, joined and knit together by every joint with which it is supplied when each part is working properly, makes bodily growth and upbuilds itself in love' (Eph. 4:16). Christ is the head of the body. If the human body is to function properly then three relationships need to be right. The first (by the nervous

system) is the relationship to the head, which issues orders
and sets the members in motion. The second is the relationship that each limb has to the whole body. Each part has to
be in the right place in relation to the body. And the third is
the relationship that each part of the body has with its
neighbouring member. There needs to be a 'joining and
knitting together'. The body will cease to function properly
and the limbs to be co-ordinated whenever the link with the
brain is damaged or severed, or if one of the limbs is injured,
or begins to act independently of the rest of the body, or if
there is a dislocation of the bones.

In an article in the magazine *New Covenant*, Derek Prince
makes some interesting observations about the function of the
muscles in the human body, which is to take the metaphor
further. He writes:[4]

> Oddly enough, muscles in the body work against each
> other. Some muscles bend my arm while others extend it.
> So it is in the body of Christ. The activities of the body
> work in tension, some bending and some extending as the
> body moves... The secret of the body's activity is the
> tensions within it. Properly balanced tensions make the
> body function. Unbalanced tensions paralyse it.

He goes on to mention some of the rightful and healthy
tensions there should be in the Church. For example, the
institutional and charismatic dimensions of the Church;
liturgical and spontaneous worship; out-going evangelism
and inner pastoral care. One might add the balance between
the past and the present, historicity and present experience,
and the perennial tension between the prophet and the priest.
God has not only set ministries in the Church. He has also
ordained certain tensions for the healthy growth and maturity of the Body — for peaceful co-existence, not discordant
conflict and division. It is always a sign of maturity in the
Church when people are prepared to accept, nay rejoice over,
these kinds of tensions and not to try to polarise the Church

around one or the other. If we do, then no wonder the Church becomes muscle-bound!

We need to recognise also that some of these tensions arise because of the kind of people we are, and since God created us we are not to complain about ourselves or anyone else. Derek Prince points out that some people are impulsive by nature. It is good to have such pioneer types, but God forbid that the whole Church and its leadership should conform to this variety of personality! There are also the cautious ones, who need the impulsive to inspire them, but who act as a healthy balance to those who want to move too fast and without consideration of all the factors involved. We find the same constructive tension between the more analytical ministry of teaching and the more inspirational ministry of prophecy. There are those who have practical minds and are good at administration, and others who could not organise to save their lives, but have most of the visions in the fellowship! All are needed, and all ought to be as committed to each other as the foot is to the leg and the leg to the body.

But there is a vital principle about commitment which we need to recognise before we can go any further. *The measure of commitment that people are prepared to make will depend on the size of the society to which they are committing themselves.* A basic fact emerges when we look at this principle, namely that *the smaller the society the greater the commitment is likely to be.* Large societies of people do not place too many demands on their adherents, and it is comparatively easy to become part of them without being too committed. Thus large churches tend to have a larger number of docile members than the smaller ones. The smallest society of all, marriage, demands a total commitment or it will never work properly.

This also needs to be seen against the background of modern man's revolt against the impersonality and anonymity of the large societies, with their faceless bureaucracies. We are back again to the Kafka type of nightmare, which is so brilliantly illustrated in his novel *The Castle*, in which K. never seems to be able to get to the source of authority. All

over the world we see this in the small minorities which are
for ever seeking independence from the larger. There are the
Scottish and Welsh Nationalists in Britain, the Provisional
I.R.A. in Ireland, the Basque Nationalists in Spain and
France, and many others who long to be free to express
themselves in a community small enough to have some
identity in a world full of large corporations which have little
or no concern for the individual. Thus the contemporary
demand for the devolution of power is both natural and
commendable, provided its object is not selfish, but is based
on the view that the smaller unit will be stronger and,
therefore, more able to make its contribution to the rest of
society. It must never become a self-perpetuating ghetto.

Howard Snyder in his book *The Problem of Wineskins, Church
Structure in a Technological Age*, expresses the view that the
small group should be the Church's basic structure. He
writes:[5]

> Today the Church needs to rediscover what the early
> Christians found, that small group meetings are something
> essential to Christian experience and growth. That the
> success of a church function is not measured by body
> count. That without the small group the church in urban
> society simply does not experience one of the most basic
> essentials of the gospel — true, rich, deep Christian
> soul-fellowship, or *koinōnia*.

He does not see it as replacing the institutional church but as
complementing it. He goes on:[6]

> Small groups can be introduced without by-passing or
> undercutting the church, although the serious incorpora-
> tion of small groups into the overall ministry of the Church
> requires some adjustments and is bound eventually to raise
> some questions about priorities. The small group is best
> seen as an essential component of the church's structure
> and ministry, not as a replacement for the church.

In the small group people can really meet each other and be committed to one another. The masks of self-deception and distrust can be removed. In 1976 when I stayed with a young Methodist minister in Huskvarna in Sweden, I noticed to the right of the front door a mask stuck to the wall near where you hung your coat. Underneath were written the words: 'Please remove your mask and be yourself!' That is not usually possible in the large group, where we can remain masked and no one need ever get to know us. But commitment in the small group is much more demanding. People will immediately notice if we are absent, and also if we are out of sorts. The strongest churches, and those most likely to grow and go on growing are those with many small groups of committed people, which are themselves, as groups, one hundred per cent committed to the larger group which they support.

We cannot in these days talk much about *commitment* before we are also talking about *community*. It seems that the Church is becoming almost obsessive about it, and, knowing the past, that is no bad thing. In the New Testament the equivalent word is no doubt *koinōnia*, translated usually by the word "fellowship". This word has been so done to death by the contemporary Church that it is another good reason for using the word community as an alternative. The basis of the Greek word *koinōnia* is a word meaning "common", which is itself derived from the Latin word *communis*, from which we get the English word "community", so that there are good grounds for using this word to translate *koinōnia*. It certainly lifts our associations away from the church-social type of meeting into a completely new atmosphere of commitment and caring. Fellowship in the New Testament can be defined as *that common sharing or participation in the grace of God, the salvation of Jesus Christ and the indwelling presence of the Holy Spirit, and the life-style that those who share in that life adopt as a result of it.* It is impossible to think of it in the New Testament without also thinking of commitment. We see this right from the start in Acts 2, when the newly blessed Christians in the aftermath of Pentecost began to share their life together. They not only prayed and worshipped together; they also shared their possessions. We are told that all who believed 'were together and had all things in common; and they sold their possessions and goods and distributed them to all, as any had need' (Acts 2:44-5). It was a theme that was to recur later in the Acts, and if we study the various ways in which the word *koinōnia* is used in the New Testament we shall notice that in the majority of texts the word is used to refer to a practical sharing of material possessions.[7] Any fellowship which excludes such considerations from its portfolio is, according to John, behaving inconsistently. 'But if anyone has the world's goods and sees his brother in need, yet closes his heart against him, how does God's love abide in him?' (1 John 3:17). No wonder Luke comments on the earliest Christian communities, 'and with great power the apostles gave their testimony to the resurrection of the Lord Jesus, and great grace was upon them all' (Acts 4:33).

This is the kind of context that ministry ought to be seen in, but the reality is, alas, often far from this pattern. Sometimes the fault lies with ministers themselves, who have little real sense of commitment to the church they are appointed to. Their attitude can be sheer professionalism. Most ministers are not trained for a team ministry, let alone for really sharing their lives with lay people. It is almost understood that ministers are a kind of class apart. One bishop in England confided in me his frustrations at trying to set up team ministries in the diocese. He told me that ministers just do not want to share their ministry with others. *Ministers have no right to demand of others what they are not prepared for themselves.* There is a need for a much greater degree of commitment of people to one another in terms of sharing life. But ministers and lay leaders have to set an example if others are to follow.

There is a fatal tendency to regard this radical commitment to one another as an optional extra for a few fanatical enthusiasts, rather than as what it should be, the normative practice of all Christians. In an interesting book which draws lessons from the great ascetic movement of the fourth century, Steve Clark shows how that movement was not regarded by its advocates as a special form of Christianity but as a renewal of basic Christian living. He writes:[8]

> The early ascetics...did not believe they were establishing a special way of life, they felt they were recapturing authentic Christianity in its primitive fervour. They considered their choice the better way, not obligatory for all Christians to be sure, but at least the choice anyone desiring a dedicated Christian life would want to make. Their goal was the renewal of basic Christian life.

Thus John Chrysostom wrote, 'In the Bible, there is no mention of monk or layman. It is men who distinguish the two... Indeed, the gospels desire all, even the married, to live as monks.'[9] If we take the Body of Christ seriously, and we are members of that Body, then total commitment to it is essential for life itself, as well as for its proper functioning and growth.

Now there may be many ways in which this commitment is expressed. For some it will mean commitment to a religious order; for others it will mean the kind of extended family community pioneered by the Church of the Redeemer, Houston, which I have described in *A New Way of Living*.[10] Another style is the Word of God Community in Ann Arbor, Michigan, which is an ecumenical para-church set-up, helping to service the Catholic Charismatic Renewal. It does not necessarily involve living under the same roof, nor in a permanent relationship with people. The question is, 'Are we committed *now*?', irrespective of how long or short a period God will lead us to be together. For all Christians a personal commitment to fellow believers in the Church we belong to is essential if one is to grow and if the Body is to function properly.

Commitment means pastoral care

If the Church today needs to rediscover the depths of commitment in which membership of the Body of Christ inevitably involves one, it also needs to find again the extent of pastoral care which is bound up in that commitment. It was Paul's ambition to proclaim Christ, 'warning every man and teaching every man in all wisdom, that we may present every man mature in Christ' (Col. 1:28). This can be said to be the goal of all pastoral care — 'to present every man mature in Christ'. Thus, we need to place alongside the newly discovered principle of "every-member ministry" the complementary principle of "every-member maturity". Paul here talks about the place of teaching in this. But pastoral responsibility in the Church should not be limited to teaching, important and central though this should be. The mind is not the only part of man's personality that needs maturing. There is, for example, our emotional life. This leads also into the area of healing, physical or psychosomatic. There are our relationships, especially in marriage and the home. The early Church did not limit pastoral care to the spiritual and the therapeutic. They cared, for example, for the widows with a "daily distribution" (Acts 6:1), whatever that was. The pastoral care to which the church needs to be committed is to the whole person, which will include his sex life as well as his prayer life, his financial affairs as well as his Bible study, his personal problems as well as his spiritual maturity. This would be a daunting task at any time, but it is even more daunting when we live in a society which has lost almost all consciousness of community, and in which the old family ties and concerns have been all but lost. Now it is a matter of every man for himself and the devil catch the hindmost. In a society based on the survival of the fittest, it is the weak and insecure who suffer most.

When we see both the need for such pastoral care and its scope we realise that any notion of a "one-man ministry" is doomed to failure. One person cannot begin to care effectively for more than a very limited number of people. *But every person in Christ needs pastoring, not least the pastor himself!* Everyone needs a person to whom one can unburden oneself. For some a spiritual director can meet that need. But even here the director is seldom on the spot, and pastoral care does, if possible, need to be integrated into the whole ministry of the local church. Here, too, the small group is at an immense advantage. In fact, it is impossible to conceive of adequate pastoral care for a large church unless it is divided up into small groups, for many pastoral needs lie hidden and masked until they are brought to the surface gently by the love and care of a small integrated body of people. It is ludicrous to think in terms of one pastor or shepherd for a huge congregation. In fact, as we have already noted, the chief role of the head pastor or shepherd should be to train others to be shepherds, so that there are enough shepherds to care adequately for the whole flock. If and when the church begins to grow, it is essential that adequate pastoral care is maintained and the number of gifted and dedicated shepherds grows also. If this does not happen, then the growth pattern of the church will not continue, and eventually the church programme will stall completely.

In recent years there has been a growing appreciation of this problem, and realistic methods have been evolved to combat it. We are beginning to see that the Church cannot be sustained by what Howard Snyder calls "the superstars". He writes, 'The Church of Jesus Christ cannot run on superstars, and God never intended that it should. There just are not that many, actually or potentially, and there never will be. God does not promise the church an affluence of superstars. But he does promise to provide all necessary leadership through the gifts of the Spirit (Eph. 4:1-16).'[11] One method which has been widely advocated is that adopted by Juan Carlos Ortiz in Argentina, and it has been called "discipling". The outline of it can be found in a book by this South American Pentecostal pastor.[12] The name is rather unfortunate, and the teaching has become tangled up with other controversial questions, but there is much good common

sense in it for all that. Ortiz gets his mandate for using the
term "discipling" from Matthew 28:19-20, where Jesus commands his followers to 'go and make disciples of all nations
...teaching them to observe all that I have commanded you'.
It seems a strange way to interpret this command to say that
Jesus tells us to make disciples for ourselves! The master-
disciple relationship is, of course, used frequently to describe
the human relationship that Jesus had with others on earth,
and, therefore, can equally describe our relationship to the
Lord today. We are still his disciples, and he is still our
master. But it is never in the New Testament used to describe
the relationship which Christians may have with one another.
The pastoral relationship we have is one of shepherds and
sheep, and we are *all* of us sheep needing shepherds. Ortiz
rightly points this out, in his own terminology, for one of the
main principles of his teaching is that no one may disciple
others who is not himself being discipled by someone else. But it
is best not to use the "discipling" terminology at all. Not only is
it biblically unsound, but it also injects into this area an
authority factor which is inappropriate, as we shall see when we
come to consider the question of authority and its relationship
to community and commitment. It would, however, be a great
pity if an argument about terminology, however important,
were to rob us of what we need to learn from Ortiz and others
about principles of sound pastoral care. What Ortiz's methods
do teach us is how any church can be divided into small enough
groups for every person to have a pastor with enough time
really to bring him to maturity. But this is something that
many have been advocating. What is special about the
experience of Ortiz in Argentina is the degree of commitment
which shepherd and sheep have to one another. In describing
this relationship he writes, 'In a discipleship relationship I do
not teach the other person to know what I know, rather I teach
him to become what I am. Discipleship then is not a
communication of knowledge, but a communication of life and
spirit.'[13] In a moving passage he tells how his church changed
from being an orphanage to being a family:[14]

So I gave my life to these disciples. I served with them. We went out to the country together. We lived together. We ate together. I opened my home to them. They came to sleep in my home. I went to sleep in their homes. Our wives started to meet together. We became like a family. And after six months...these people were so changed that the whole orphanage noticed it... It took us almost three years, but we finally...changed our orphanage into a family.

One might be reading again the story of the renewal of the Church of the Redeemer, Houston, which followed a similar pattern. Another person who describes the same principle is Bob Girard, minister of Our Heritage Wesleyan Church in Scottsdale, Arizona:[15]

Step 1: gather a few men.
Step 2: live with them (so they can see you as you are).
Step 3: pour your life into them.
Step 4: teach them all you know (as they are ready for it, they'll let you know by *asking*. And the Spirit will also let you know).
Step 5: show them how.
Step 6: let them learn by experience (even by failures).

This seems to be a very effective way of shepherding people today and programming the Church into a real growth pattern. It was Paul's method, too, if we read 2 Timothy 2:2, 'What you have heard from me before many witnesses entrust to faithful men who will be able to teach others also.'

Commitment means submission

The words "authority" and "submission" are as unpopular today as the word "commitment". There is some good reason for this. The world has seen the effects of Fascist and Communist dictatorships. It has seen where the abuse of authority has led to. It stills sees it today in the growing number of police states which are ruled by force rather than consent. The Church, too, is only beginning to rid itself of its past authoritarianism. It is difficult to forget the cruelty of Crusades and Inquisition, the heresy trials, the death of Servetus at the stake, prosecuted by none other than John Calvin for the heinous offence of, amongst other things, denying infant baptism. In the *Institutes* Calvin reminds people that there were those who hated the very word *discipline*. In the light of what happened to Servetus, it is understandable! But today the pendulum has swung too far in the opposite direction.

If we end, as we must, with the consideration of submission in relationship to commitment, then we need to remember where we began, with the only option — love. Submission easily becomes harsh and tyrannical if it does not spring from the motive of love and is not exercised in the spirit of love.

It is very important, right at the beginning of any consideration of authority, that we see it at two levels. First, there is that authority which Christ alone has as Head of the Body, the Church, and which he has delegated to no one. Jesus said to the disciples, 'All authority in heaven and on earth has been given to me' (Matt. 28:18). It is an authority which is expressed, too, in the working of the Holy Spirit. The gifts of the Holy Spirit, for instance, are inspired and apportioned by the Holy Spirit 'to each one individually as he wills' (1 Cor. 12:11). It was the Holy Spirit who issued the authoritative command, 'Set apart for me Barnabas and Saul for the work to which I have called them' (Acts 13:1). As in the human body, the head is in control and issues the instructions, and every part of the body is linked with the head by the marvellous nervous system. No person on earth, be he apostle, pope or archbishop, may usurp this divine authority. But there is another authority, which some have over others in the Body of Christ. This is not a human authority. It also comes from God, but it is delegated to man, and is held by him in trust, to be exercised in subordination to the overriding authority of God himself, and in loving service of those to whom he ministers in the name of Christ.

Now the balance between these two authorities is most important and closely related. Because we are to be one Body it is not always possible to see where one begins and the other ends. If one or the other is stressed there are dangers. Protestantism has tended to stress the former. It has sometimes been called "the right of private judgment". It is the assertion that every child of God has the right of private access to God. We do not have to go through an intermediary other than Christ himself. The danger of this, when it is stressed and not related to the other kind of authority, is that it leads all too easily to individualism and a false kind of pietism, the hot-line-to-heaven way of thinking, and often introduces an element of anarchy into the church situation. Everyone "doing his own thing" may give pleasure to some, but it is self-deceptive and encourages pride and vainglory.

However, there are also dangers when stress is put on the delegated authority of the Church. Roman Catholicism has tended in this direction. Roman Catholics until comparatively recently have not been encouraged in their personal and individual life with God, other than in a strictly devotional sense. Catholicism is greatly afraid of illuminism, and has tended to encourage a form of authority which has kept the laity in particular in its place. Both emphases lead to immaturity. A person whose life is almost solely a personal relationship with God develops all kinds of emotional problems and extreme ideas, whereas the person who never seems to be able to get past the person next to him and into the presence of God himself remains inert and immature. Both emphases are a real denial of man's individuality and humanity, and both produce unfortunate stereotypes. Commitment to others in the Body of Christ needs to be seen as the freeing of a person's individuality, which can only happen in a free relationship to God *and* to our fellow believers. True submission secures freedom; it does not take it away. Indeed it is the very freedom so many are looking for and can't find because submission is the last place where they would expect to find it. True Christian maturity is to be found on the one hand in a healthy relationship to God, which is not dependent entirely on one's relationship to others, and which does draw continuous inspiration from Him, and on the other in an equally healthy relationship with our fellow-believers, which is open to hearing and seeing God in them, and a submission to both. In other words we need *both* kinds of authority, and wisdom to know which is which. At the same time we have to remember that the Church is a family not an army, and so, while the imagery of warfare is useful to describe the spiritual battle, and is employed as such in the New Testament, it is out of place as a description of the relationship that exists between Christians.

In view of the present absence of discipline and authority in Western society, in vivid contrast to the rigid way of life in Communist countries, we need to be careful that we do not react too sharply and impose a rigid authority and a new hierarchy or chain of command. The Christian is called to a much more difficult approach, for he must avoid both anarchy and tyranny, individualism and a corporateness which denies to the individual room to be himself, and for his personality to blossom. Where communities have succeeded in getting this right, they are just about the most wholesome societies you can find on this earth, and it is to this balance that the whole Christian Church is called.

It is when we examine the life and ministry of Paul that we see how authority should be exercised. Paul possessed an authority which no one today has. He was an apostle of Christ. If you like, he was one of the founder members of the Christian Church. In the light of this, it is interesting to note the way he exercised this authority. In his book *Why Priests?* Hans Küng draws out the importance of this:[16]

Paul was never afraid to bring his authority into play. Yet it is characteristic of the Spirit of Christ that impelled Paul, that he did not exploit his mandatory power...

Instead he always voluntarily restricted the exercise of his mandate in the conviction that the apostles were not lords and masters of the faith, but initiators of the joy of belief in all members of the community; that his churches belonged not to him but to the Lord; and that their members were free in the Spirit, called to be free and not slaves of men... For Paul, liberty is the basic datum which he respects, and struggles for, so that his communities may follow him not out of constraint and force, but freely. Of course, where there was a risk of abandonment of Christ and his gospel in favour of another gospel, he had to use the threat of anathema and excommunication. But what he did in regard to an individual (temporary excommunication in the hope of an improvement) he never practised in respect of a community, even in cases of major deviations. *Paul was always very careful* to avoid using his mandatory power. Instead of issuing prohibitions, he appealed to individuals' judgment and responsibility. Instead of using constraint, he sought to convince. Instead of imposing himself, he exhorted. He said 'we...' not 'you...'; he did not issue sanctions but used forgiveness; and ultimately did not stifle but stimulated freedom.

In other words he treated those to whom he wrote as adults not as children, as equals not as disciples, and as brothers not as servants. Even when he had rights, he chose not to use them. When he does use his divinely authorised mandate, he does so to edify and instruct rather than to destroy. We, who have considerably less authority than Paul, would do well to follow his example. Dietrich Bonhoeffer writes of this hankering for a false kind of authority:[17]

Its root is a desire to re-establish some sort of immediacy, a dependence upon human beings in the Church. Genuine authority knows that all immediacy is especially baneful in matters of authority. Genuine authority realises that it can exist only in the service of him who alone has authority...

It is bound...by the saying of Jesus: 'One is your Master, even Christ, and all ye are brethren' (Matt. 23:8).[17]

In his book *Jesus and the Spirit*, James Dunn draws this out still further.[18] He shows how it was the community as a whole which possessed authority in the early Church. Although, perhaps, he presses this too far, for clearly there was, as we shall be seeing, a structured and authoritative ministry in each local church, nevertheless it is important not to overdo the authority that the local elders may have possessed. Dunn points out, for example, that Paul never addresses himself to a leadership group within a community, apart possibly from Philippians 1:1, and even there he includes the saints with the leaders. His instructions and exhortations are generally addressed to the community as a whole. Paul's stress is on every member exercising his gifts. The ministry of admonishing, judging, comforting and teaching is not the prerogative of a chosen few (see Rom. 15:14; 1 Cor. 5:4f. 2 Cor. 2:7; Col. 3:16; 1 Thess. 5:14). As Dunn shows, 'Even Paul himself does not hesitate to submit his opinions to them... The "Amen" which the congregation utters after a prayer or prophecy is not just a formal liturgical assent: it indicates rather the importance Paul attaches to the community's members being able to understand and to give assent to what is said in its worship.'[19]

In his conclusions James Dunn[20] sees authority in the Pauline communities as one of

ongoing dialectic between the more formal authority of apostle as apostle and the kerygmatic tradition on the one hand, and the charismatic authority of all ministry within the community and of the community itself on the other; between the individual with his word or act containing its authority within itself as *charisma*, and the community with its responsibility to test and evaluate all *charismata*; between the decisive salvation-history events of the past (resurrection appearance commissioning and kerygmatic tradition) and the new situations, problems and demands requiring new revelations and fresh interpretation of the tradition. This vision of the charismatic mutual inter-dependence and dynamic interaction of both ministry and authority is a striking one; its realisation would clearly depend on a sensitiveness to the direction of the Spirit and a deliberate restraint on self-assertiveness on the part of all members of the community at all times.

We began this chapter with the only option open to God's people; *to love one another*. It would be a pity to end it with the stark word *authority*. Understood and used properly, authority is essential for the healthy maturing of the Church. But it has also been used as an excuse for most of the vile things that man has done to man through the centuries. William Barclay shows that the word *exousia* in secular Greek developed a bad meaning. '*Exousia*, the power, the rank, the place, the prestige, the abundance a man possesses may produce in him a certain arrogance which is connected with *hubris*, the pride which despises man and defies God.'[21] There is more than a touch of this in the Jewish leaders' demand of Jesus, 'By what authority are you doing these things, and who gave you this authority?' (Matt. 21:23). The word *commitment* also has harsh overtones to it. It can be another word for the quest which some may have for power, and their desire to rule over others. It is only one step to the practice of dividing churches into the committed and the uncommitted, members and non-members, with the judg-ment of others which this inevitably involves.

We need to remember that Jesus Christ did not come basically to give some people authority over others, but to set all men free to serve one another. He came to save us from our sinful domineering natures and to set men free from slavery to one another. 'For freedom Christ has set us free,' Paul wrote to the Galatians, 'stand fast therefore and do not submit again to a yoke of slavery' (Gal. 5:1). He gave us no option but to love one another, and our commitment and submission to one another should spring from that love, or else it is an evil thing which will corrupt and destroy us.

10

Is There a Blueprint?

WE HAVE BEEN concerned so far almost exclusively with the question of the *function* of the ministry, not with the matter of titles and offices. This does appear to be the New Testament emphasis. Jesus Christ was far more concerned with the quality of a person's life and what he did with it in terms of ministry, than with what that person might be called, and what kind of status or authority he might have in relationship to the rest of the community. When Jesus spoke to Peter about his future ministry in Matthew 16 he gave him a new name not a new title, and that name said as much about his character as it did about his office. However, the New Testament does refer to those who exercised a ministry of leadership in the churches. Paul appointed elders (Acts 14:23) and wrote to Timothy concerning the qualities to look for in setting apart people for various ministries. When he writes to the Philippians he includes in the general salutation to them the bishops and deacons (Phil. 1:1).

But before we can go on to consider the kind of leadership we should be looking for in the local and universal Church, we ought to deal with an important question of interpretation: namely, how far are we to take the New Testament as a blueprint for the Church of today? Do the scriptures which refer to ministry in the Church, for example, have the same kind of timeless authority as those which refer to the death and resurrection of Christ?

We need to remember that just as the nature of Jesus was both divine and human, so the nature of the scriptures has a divine and a human aspect, and we need to make allowance for both. Those scholars who put the letters attributed to Paul through the computer and deduce, on the basis of style and use of words, that some were his and some were not, tend to neglect the divine element of inspiration which was a major factor in the writing of the New Testament. On the other hand, those who believe that it was almost dictated from heaven deny the human element which led to its writing. To understand the Bible we need to see both these elements and the balance between them, and especially we need the Holy Spirit to guide us in our understanding and interpretation of them. Above all, we need to beware of that simplistic sentence 'It is the clear teaching of scripture', which one hears so often, even when the meaning is anything but clear. Dogmatism in such circumstances is out of place.

We need also to distinguish in the Bible between what is a fixed and unalterable truth — which does not change either in the course of time or in the context of cultural variety — and where the passage is describing how the Holy Spirit inspired people in an *ad hoc* situation. In this latter instance, we are not to follow slavishly how people were led *then*, but to learn from the example of their response to the guidance of the Spirit, and expect ourselves to be led by the same Spirit, though perhaps in a quite different manner. In other words we have to distinguish between what is exemplary in scripture and what is mandatory. To give an example of what we mean, let us take what the New Testament has to say about apostles and bishops. It has a lot to say about apostles, and regards them as possessing a vital function in the ministry of the Church. Paul actually writes, 'First apostles' (1 Cor. 12:28). On the other hand, there is no office in the New Testament that approximates to the modern bishop. The word *episcopos* is there, but it is simply a synonym for the word *presbuteros*, translated 'elder'. But today we have few who would claim to be apostles, but several Churches which have bishops. If we were to follow slavishly the New Testament we should be looking earnestly for apostles, and looking askance at our bishops. In chapter 12 we shall be tracing the reasons why the Church so quickly dropped apostles and accepted episcopacy. But it is all wrong if you go strictly by the letter of the law.

If the New Testament is our blueprint for ministry in the Church, all one can say is that it is a strange blueprint. There is a certain haphazardness about the appointments to office in the New Testament which only makes sense if you view them as the *ad hoc* promptings of the Holy Spirit, amidst the most taxing of circumstances. The Church was having to make adjustments all the time. It was growing rapidly and spreading widely. It was crossing all kinds of racial, social and cultural frontiers. It was often under fire from its enemies. It had to make, at times, radical adjustments to rapidly changing situations. This was to go on for many years beyond the first century when the New Testament was being written. It was having to face increasingly complex moral and theological controversies, and to define faith and ethics in order to establish some kind of norm. The emergence of what has been called 'monepiscopacy' so early and so quickly, and the universal acceptance of it throughout the Church, taking into account the stress which the Church was going through at the time, is truly amazing and convincing. But its appearance can hardly be described as "scriptural" in the strict sense of "office", although as we shall see in terms of "function" it is truly in line with those mandatory principles which are established in the New Testament as norms for all time.

The New Testament writers, it would seem, are not interested in establishing a blueprint. They are more concerned with "life" than with defining too closely how the Church should be governed and who should do what. For instance, those who attempt to find the origins of the order of deacons in Acts 6 have a hard time proving it. Here is an *ad hoc* situation, and the Church responding sensibly to it. To establish the order of deacons here is to read back into scripture what was not there originally. In any case, Stephen very soon began to behave like an apostle (no doubt because the Holy Spirit led him to), and he lost his life as a result. Another of the seven, Philip, was soon fulfilling the function of an evangelist, while someone probably filled in for him in his role of looking after the widows. We see no stereotype here, but flexibility to the movings of the Holy Spirit. We have already noticed how freely Paul uses the word "deacon" in 1 Timothy while at the same time referring to a separate ministry; in the same epistle he refers to himself and Timothy as deacons. Even the word "apostle" is used so freely that it is not easy to define the office as it was understood in the New Testament. It seems that almost anyone from the exalted position of a Paul to a lowly messenger boy could at times be called an "apostle".

What in effect we do, if we make the New Testament into a blueprint, is to wrest the scriptures by reading into them our own ideas and viewpoints. We also put them into cold storage. We try to "freeze" them in the first century and re-create "New Testament" churches. It's like a rich American who sees an old house in England and loves it so much he has it moved, stone by stone, to his own country and re-erected there, totally out of its context. The Holy Spirit won't let us do this. We cannot freeze the Church at the first century or any other century, however much it may appeal to us. A Church may pride itself on being "Reformed", but if it is really building itself on the pattern of the sixteenth and seventeenth centuries it will be an unattractive anachronism. It is foolish to make no allowance, when building a doctrine of the ministry, for post-testamental developments. We have especially seen how important this is in the area of the ministry of women. If we "freeze" the Church in the New Testament, then there is much richness of life which we will have to deny, to the detriment of all and the derogation of the Holy Spirit.

In the book *Christ's Living Body*, edited by John P. Baker, Roger Beckwith seeks to answer the question: is the New Testament pattern of ministry *exemplary* or is it *mandatory*? If it is merely exemplary, it is still not to be despised, for the examples of the New Testament were 'written for our learning' (1 Cor. 10:11). Roger Beckwith, after mentioning some features (like the appointment of deacons) which he regards as exemplary, lists three features of New Testament ministry which he regards as mandatory:[1]

1.   Paul's doctrine of the Church as the Body of Christ in which each member has his own important office or ministry. The spiritual gifts are for *all*.

2.   Certain ministries are given by Christ to the Church to equip Christians for their own ministries. Roger Beckwith regards the appointment of elders as mandatory in New Testament times, and the apostles endeavoured to make it universal throughout the Church, thus making it mandatory still.

3.   The *plurality of elders* is also mandatory.

In an interesting working paper in preparation for the 1977 National Evengelical Anglican Congress at Nottingham University, J. Andrew Kirk has drawn up his own list of outstanding facets of the ministry of the Apostolic Church. Concisely they are:

1.   No distinction either in form, language or theory between clergy and laity was ever accepted by the New Testament Church.

2.   The ministry is co-extensive with the entire church (1 Cor. 12:7).

3.   The local church in the apostolic age always functioned under a plurality of leadership.

4.   There are no uniform models for ministry in the New Testament; the patterns are flexible and versatile.

5.   In the New Testament church can be found both leadership and authority, but no kind of hierarchical structure.

6.   There is one, and only one, valid distinction which the New Testament appears to recognise within the ministry, apart from the different functions to which we have been alluding: the distinction between *local* and *itinerant* ministries.

Andrew Kirk's list is set in the context of the hermeneutical task with which this chapter is also concerned. He seeks in the light of this to distinguish between those timeless principles which are appropriate at any time and in any age, and those features which are temporary or cultural and exemplary. This task is one which every age has to engage in. But we undertake it with daunting odds against us: namely, the innate conservatism of religious people. What may be for some a more important task is to discover the meaning of the Church in its contemporary setting, for, as we have already seen, the ministry exists for the Church, not the Church for the ministry. If we do not get our understanding of the Church right, there is no hope that we shall get the ministry right.

Andrew Kirk in his paper warns us about this task:

The Church must consciously be on its guard to distinguish between what is genuinely a theological norm and what has become normative by extended use and the uncreative inability to see new possibilities. The contemporary challenge of the world to the Church's mission may, therefore, be a valid tool by which we can 'unmask' as *cultural accretions* that which the Church has tended to accept as binding doctrine. Particularly in England, we need to be sensitive to the ambiguities and errors of the doctrinal, ethical and structural formation of the Church over a long period of unchallenged alliance with the middle class.

It is those who most fervently lay claim to being a "New Testament Church" who need to heed these warnings as much as anyone. They are in danger of confusing what they claim to be biblical norms with ecclesiastical tradition on the one hand, and middle-class culture on the other. Our hermeneutical task is not an easy one, but we are bound to undertake it, and to sift what is of permanent and enduring value from a mass of accretions which are of only secondary importance. The urgency of what we have to do is accentuated by the apparently inexorable drift away from the organised

structured churches, either into independent church structures — which adds immensely to the difficulties of Christian
unity and introduces new divides which were not there before
— or into heathenism, the darkness of unbelief which is
extinguishing the light of the gospel of Jesus Christ throughout the Western world. We must not panic or be stampeded
into reckless surgery which could well cut out more living
than diseased "tissue" in the Body of Christ. It calls for skill,
patience, gentleness and compassion. But it also calls for
action. The wind of change is in the air, and when it is the
wind of the Spirit, we dare not ignore what he wants to say to
us, nor through fear draw back from what he wants us to do.

Part III

The Church and its Leaders

Introduction

LEADERSHIP IN THE CHURCH

WE HAVE LEFT the question of leadership until last — not because it is unimportant, but because it can only properly be understood *after* a consideration of what ministry is itself and what the Church is — for which ministry alone exists. We have already said that we are deliberately avoiding the technical titles, so that we can major on that which primarily distinguishes certain people from others in the Body of Christ. They are "leaders", though in different Churches they may be called "bishops", "priests", "ministers", "pastors", "presbyters" or "deacons". We move, of course, into a much more controversial area. It is easy simply to write about "ministry", but nearer the rub when we come to talk about "offices" and people who have a position of leadership and, therefore, authority over others. We come into head-on confrontation with the Church as it has evolved, and as it is at present ordered. But we can take comfort. It would be a strange conclusion to reach that the Church has been radically wrong for two thousand years, and, therefore, needs a completely new structure. In fact, the conclusions the author has come to are that all the basic ingredients are present in the Church today, and that the main issue lies in a rediscovery of what ministry is all about, and in the light of this a re-adjustment of the present ordained ministry to conform with the New Testament principles. But in case one is concluding from this that the next chapters are a whitewash, let it be made clear that the changes needed are still radical. They ought to begin in the hearts and minds of the present leaders of the Church, and especially need to be transmitted in the whole training programme of the Church, which should be adjusted as a result. Above all, the Church ought to be exorcised of the demon of professionalism, so that the old distinction between a professional full-time ministry and an amateur part-time one is eradicated once and for all, and it needs to be seen that the only distinction allowed to be made is between those who have been called to be leaders (with varying degrees of commitment and responsibility) and those who haven't, recognising that *all* are called to minister and be ministered to in the Body of Christ.

In chapter 11 we shall be considering leadership in the local church; in chapter 12, leadership in the larger universal Church and the relationship which it should have to the local church; finally, in chapter 13, we shall take a look at leadership itself, how it arises, what one should be looking for in a leader, and how leaders are set apart or "ordained" for their ministry.

In previous chapters, in our efforts to stress (as I believe the New Testament does) the importance of *service*, and of *function* in the Body of Christ, we may have given an impression that leadership is of little importance. It may have been deduced from what has been written that the only thing that matters is what we do and how we do it. Certainly, as we read Dietrich Bonhoeffer's book *Life Together* and James Dunn's *Jesus and the Spirit,* an impression is left that the New Testament Church was so much a "Servant Church" or a charismatic community that it was only a trivial detail that there were leaders at all. James Dunn's contention is that charismatic ministry, which was largely leaderless and was the Pauline ideal, gave way later to a more limited recognised ministry.[1] He suggests that by the time the Pastoral Epistles had been written[2]

The vision of charismatic community has faded, ministry

and authority have become the prerogative of the few, the experience of the Christ-Spirit has lost its vitality, the preservation of the past has become more important than openness to the present and future. *Spirit and charisma have become in effect subordinate to office, to ritual, to tradition — early-Catholicism indeed!* (Italics mine).

James Dunn allows for what he calls the "Johannine alternative" — the final *cri de coeur* of the last living apostle for the glorious liberties of charismatic ministry. But one wonders whether he has not got it a bit too black-and-white, and whether the role of leadership was in fact stronger in the charismatic community than he is prepared to allow, and whether he has deduced rather too much from the contrast between the earlier Pauline corpus and the Pastoral Epistles.

Lastly, before we can consider the subject of leadership we need to clarify one important point. In the New Testament, leadership in the local church was obviously dominated by the concept of elders (*presbuteroi*) or bishops (*episcopoi*), and these two words were used interchangeably. It is comparatively easy to make the big jump from the local church in the first century to the local church in the twentieth and still see today a pattern of eldership being worked out in much the same way as it was in the early Church. But when we come to consider trans-local leadership which goes beyond the local church, we have many difficulties and differences of opinion. We can use the word "elder" without too much difficulty or ambiguity, and different denominations have different nomenclature for their forms of local leadership. But as we shall be using the word "bishop" a great deal in our consideration of trans-local leadership, this calls for some explanation, especially as for some it is a highly emotive word. My main reasons for using it, and for spending some time on the matter of the evolution of episcopacy in the first and second centuries, are two. First, with regard to the *past*. Episcopacy has been the dominant form of trans-local leadership from the beginning of the second century until the

Reformation, and, of course, in much of the divided Church since the sixteenth century. Secondly, with regard to the *future*. It is inconceivable that any united Church will not incorporate episcopacy. However, if there are those who have scruples about this, they are free to substitute whatever other word they feel is proper, provided that they believe there is a place for trans-local leadership anyway. Certainly no one can take trans-local leadership seriously without having a hard look at the origins of episcopacy. Here the New Testament does not help us too much. The Church had not developed fully enough during the period when the New Testament was being written for trans-local leadership to have evolved. There are some seeds of it in the New Testament. Even the apostles did not exercise the kind of role the bishops were later to have, since their authority seems to have extended only over the churches they had actually founded, and, as we shall see, the apostles were a special order, the founding fathers of the Church, and no attempt was seriously made to replace the original apostles after they had died. But, to re-assure, we shall be treating bishops as the "elders" of the universal Church, not as authoritarian prelates, which, alas, many were to become and so to depart from the pattern of pastoral service of which there are several splendid models in the New Testament.

Finally, before we turn to consider leadership in both the local setting and the larger one of the universal Church, it is important to see the similarities between these two aspects. In the local church there are the elders, one of whom is the "leader-president", or a kind of "bishop" of the local church. In the universal Church there are the various "leader-presidents" of the local churches, who can meet together as a kind of "college" or trans-local core group for leadership, and their "leader-president" is in effect the bishop as we now know him. You can take it a stage further, and have the core group or "college" of bishops, who have their "leader-president" or archbishop. Protestants must not shirk the logic of where this ultimately takes them. I must leave this to the reader's imagination. But it should not be an hierarchical structure as such, for each "leader-president" shares power with several others. There is no one person who is ever above others. At every level the "leader-president" is only a *primus inter pares*.

When we look at it like this, we can see that the present structure of our churches is not all that different. But there is still a need, as we shall see, for some radical re-adjustments and changes in personal attitudes if the system is going to work properly. And no system, however perfect it may be, will work if people are not willing for it to do so.

11

Leadership in the Local Church

WHEN WE LOOK at the New Testament for a pattern of leadership in the local church, we are confronted again and again with elders, who were appointed to each new church shortly after it had been founded by the apostles. In Acts 14:23 we are told that Paul and Barnabas appointed elders for them 'in every church'. It would seem clear from the fact that they are mentioned so frequently that it was the standard practice in New Testament times to do this. The old Jewish presbyteral system was taken over without apology.

Now before we go any further there are three important matters relative to elders which need to be mentioned:

1. The words translated "elder" or "presbyter" and "bishop" or "overseer", namely *presbuteros* and *episcopos*, are synonyms in the New Testament, and both are used to describe the same office. Jerome wrote about this, 'Among the ancients bishops and presbyters are the same, for the one is a term of dignity, the other of age.' The arguments from which this fact is deduced are too well established to repeat them here. They can be found in several modern books and in Bishop Lightfoot's commentary on Philippians.[1]

2. Elders are usually mentioned in the plural in the New Testament. There are only four exceptions. In 1 Timothy 3:2 and Titus 1:7 the bishop appears in the singular. But it seems clear that this is a generalising singular. There is also

the rather obscure use of the singular in 2 John 1 and 3 John 1. Here it is likely that John had acquired what Michael Green calls 'the affectionate title of respect' as the outstanding Christian teacher of his generation.[2]

3. The word "elder" does imply an older person. It does not necessarily mean an old person, but neither can it refer to a young person. Unlike our own times, the ancient world always held age in respect. The Greek governing body was called the *gerousia,* which is derived from the word for an old man. The Romans had their *senatus,* from the Latin word for an old man. In England we have our *alderman* and the Arabs their *sheik*, both words which mean an old person. Whilst this need not be a hard and fast rule, the implications are clear that normally older rather than younger people are eligible for Christian leadership. A. E. Harvey in an article on "elders" has argued that our basic understanding of *presbuteroi* should be governed by the meaning "oldermen" and, it was these men who led the early Christian communities and later the episcopate.[3] But we need flexibility here, too, for Paul wrote to Timothy, 'Let no one despise your youth' (1 Tim. 4:12). Timothy was not, so far as we know, an elder. But he had a position of responsibility and an itinerant ministry. In some of his epistles Paul links Timothy's name with his own (e.g. 2 Corinthians, Philippians, Colossians).

Of the importance of elders in the world of the first century there is no doubt. They had a long history in Judaism, and there is mention of them in Egypt (Gen. 50:7) and in Moab and Midian (Num. 22:7). They were there in the days of Jewish slavery in Egypt (Exod. 3:16) and during the Exodus (Exod. 19:7, 24:1). They had a special place when the seventy were appointed to assist Moses in leadership (Num. 11:16). They were equally prominent in the Graeco-Roman world. In fact, it would have been most surprising if the Christian Church had not appointed elders, so common were they throughout the world as leaders of both religious and secular life. Their importance in the early Church can be gauged by the part they played in the council of Jerusalem (Acts 15). The elders there were united with the apostles in the consideration of the issues involved. When at the end of the conference Judas and Silas, who were prophets, were issued with the encyclical to take to the churches, it was clearly stated that it came from 'the brethren, *both the apostles and the elders*' (v. 23). Throughout this chapter the apostles and elders are linked together as if possessing a common authority. Their position of importance in the early Church is clearly established by this account of what was obviously a moment of considerable significance. Jerusalem was regarded as a kind of headquarters of the Church, a position it held until the fearful siege and destruction of the city in A.D. 70 which is so graphically described by the Jewish historian Josephus. When Paul returned to Jerusalem later in his life, and was received by the Church, he had an appointment with James, the Lord's brother, and we are told 'all the elders were present' (Acts 21:18).

The role of elders

Elders were appointed in the churches for a number of functions. They were to exercise authority or to rule (1 Tim. 5:17). They were to 'care for God's Church' (1 Tim. 3:5). Peter exhorts them to 'tend the flock of God that is your charge' (1 Pet. 5:2). And, since Peter goes on to tell the younger Christians to 'be subject to the elders' (5:5), he clearly has in mind that elders will have authority over others. In Hebrews 13:17, although the word "elders" is not used, they are clearly in mind when the writer says, 'Obey your leaders and submit to them; for they are keeping watch over your souls, as men who will have to give account.' Elders are those who "watch over" the spiritual lives of men and women, and will one day have to give an account of their stewardship. Paul says that they are to be respected and 'esteemed very highly in love because of their work' (1 Thess. 5:12). In Acts 20:28 Paul tells the elders at Ephesus that the Holy Spirit has made them "overseers" or "bishops" (*episcopous*). 'In the ancient world the elders were the backbone of every community,' writes William Barclay, 'and it was so in the Church.'[4] So universal is this pattern in the New Testament that we find elders holding a prominent position in John's vision of heaven, where the twenty-four elders symbolise the leadership of the united Old and New Covenant Churches. They worship God continually before the throne of the Lamb (Rev. 4:4; 5:8; 11:16; 19:4).

But elders had other functions too, of which the most important was teaching. There would be some (not all) who laboured in "preaching and teaching" (1 Tim. 5:17). They needed to be "apt" in teaching (1 Tim. 3:22), and to 'hold firm to the sure word as taught, so that [they] may be able to give instruction in sound doctrine and also to confute those who contradicted it' (Titus 1:9). They are to 'feed the Church of the Lord' (Acts 20:28). Another function was pastoral care. They were pastors who were to 'tend the flock of God' (1 Pet. 5:2). They were also to heal the sick (Jas. 5:14). In addition they were to engage in evangelism, and the reference to the fact that an elder must be 'well thought of by outsiders' (1 Tim. 3:7) is significant in this context. Although the chief role of the elders was church-orientated, evangelism was not to be neglected. And when Paul encourages the elders of Ephesus concerning his own ministry, he tells them that he had testified 'both to Jews and to Greeks of repentance to God and of faith in our Lord Jesus Christ' (Acts 20:21). He clearly expected them to follow his example in this area as well as in that of pastoral concern and leadership in the church. The elders, too, are to have a correcting or admonishing ministry. Paul tells the Ephesian elders that for three years he had not ceased 'night or day to admonish every one with tears' (Acts 20:31).

What, in other words, we are to expect in the leaders or elders of each church is the five-fold ministry described in Ephesians 4:11. One leader may be more accomplished or gifted in the ministry of prophecy, whereas another may be more a teacher. Another may have evangelistic gifts. Another may have apostolic gifts, another pastoral. The five-fold ministry will not be limited to the leaders. Other members of the church may have ministries too, but not the charism or gift of leadership. It is this particular charism which distinguishes the leader from the rest. Incidentally, if we are to cling closely to the philology of the New Testament and call the leaders "elders", then, according to Alan Cole, we shall have to call the rest "idiots"! For the Greek word *idiotes* is used to describe a person who does not hold any official position in the church.[5] For obvious reasons it would be better not to call such people anything! They are brethren or saints and that is all that matters, and they are equally involved and committed to ministry in the church, although theirs does not happen to be leadership.

One role which the New Testament says nothing about is that of leading worship or presiding at the Lord's Supper or the Eucharist. It is not without significance that John sees the elders in heaven worshipping the Lamb, not conducting a worship service! It is an indication of how far our own present practice of ministry has wandered from the norms of the New Testament that almost the major and definitive function of the ordained ministry is conducting services and, particularly in Roman Catholic and Anglican churches, celebrating Holy Communion or the Eucharist. The New Testament is entirely silent on this, and it would seem from 1 Corinthians that the earliest Christian worship was a free-for-all, each person making his own contribution (see particularly, 1 Cor. 14:26). When there were disorders in worship and the Lord's Supper, Paul does not address himself to the leaders, or establish any norms for the leadership of such gatherings, but to the "brethren" and the church at large. A church which is filled and guided by the Spirit needs little guidance and control in worship. In a church which is quenching the Spirit and is largely devoid of his influence, the leaders have to rely much more on a carefully prepared order of service, without allowing for spontaneous and free expressions of worship which come with the manifesting of charismatic gifts, and the other contributions of a spiritually alive congregation. When

Paul and others use the word *leitourgos* of ministers (from which we get the English word "liturgy"), they are not referring to a single person taking a service, but to the priesthood of all believers, 'offering spiritual sacrifices acceptable to God through Jesus Christ' (1 Pet. 2:5).[6] J. W. Charley in his commentary on the Anglican/Roman Catholic Statement on Ministry and Ordination (1973) says, 'The New Testament itself tells us nothing about who should preside (at the Eucharist).'[7] But the Agreed Statement itself states that, because it is the central act of Christian worship, 'It is right that he who has oversight in the church and is the focus of the unity should preside at the celebration of the eucharist.'[8] If, however, you examine the Agreed Statement it is assumed that there is one minister. The plurality of eldership is not in view. Perhaps for Roman Catholics this is somewhat covered by the practice of con-celebration. This is commendable in that it helps to loosen the concept of the one-man ministry. But only ordained priests can celebrate, and so in most churches we are back to the "professionals" celebrating. Michael Green suggests the practice in the Congregational Church of having a layman presiding at the eucharist once a year to show that it can be done without the roof collapsing in protest.[9] But that is rather artificial. It really ought to be a ministry which any elder or leader can exercise, whether he is officially ordained or not. Alternatively, bishops could, as we shall be mentioning later, ordain the senior laity for ministry in the local church. It is a lamentable situation that a minister today, when for instance he goes away on holiday, has to import another ordained person from another church to take the Communion service, while there are dedicated and effective lay leaders, well able to do this, sitting idly in the pews.

It remains to say something about how, practically speaking, these concepts of Christian leadership can be grafted on to the present set-up in our churches. There are obvious difficulties. But there is no reason why the leadership of the church cannot be shared amongst a number of leaders, of whom the minister is the one who normally would be the president or chairman. It does not need an Act of Parliament, but an act of grace on the part of the minister to "give over" and allow the charismatically gifted lay leaders to share with him in the ministry of leadership. It has been attempted with varying degrees of success in a number of traditionally one-man-leadership orientated churches. Where there are the charisms of the Spirit and the willingness of the minister to share his leadership with others, it works perfectly well without causing disruption or schism or giving the bishop ulcers. In the book *Christ's Living Body*, John Baker gives five examples, each with a slightly different approach to suit the local situation, and in every instance the bishop co-operates and gives his official sanction to what is being done. In some cases the bishop has actually commissioned the lay elders for their task.[10] In his book *Ordained Elders and Renewal Communities*, Stephen Clark shows how this situation was dealt with in the ascetic movement in the fourth century, which gave birth to monasticism.[11] The renewed Christians banded together into communities, and appointed elders to lead them, who were unordained but exercised in every respect (apart from celebrating the eucharist) the role of leadership which the ordained were exercising in the Church at large. As the communities grew in size and influence it was increasingly important that they should be kept within the structure of the larger Church, and this was simply expedited by the bishops ordaining the most senior of the unordained elders. Even Anthony the Great, one of the pioneers of early monasticism, lived and functioned in every way as an elder, yet all the evidence indicates that he was not ordained. And Pachomius, who pioneered a new pastoral system, was not only unordained but actually resisted ordination out of humility.[12]

When a church begins to grow, and especially when the growth rate is fast, there is an immediate need for wise leadership. The traditional approaches to leadership cannot supply this need. If something is not done about it, there is a real danger of schism. The story of a church in England supports this point. When a deeper work of the Holy Spirit began in this church, one of the results that followed was the development of powerful and indigenous lay leadership. The church grew in numbers and in maturity and increasingly the minister allowed his rapidly maturing lay leaders to exercise their charismatic gifts of leadership in the church. He trained them and prepared them for this. When the time came for the minister to leave, the church was moving along so well that they hardly missed his departure, and during a long interregnum the church continued to prosper. Under these circumstances the bishop could well have said, 'The church is going on so well, we don't need to appoint a successor, but I will come and ordain one or two of the leading laymen.' The "system" is such that it probably never occurred to anyone that this was a possibility. But why not? We do need to consider seriously whether it is always for the best to import a stranger into a position of supreme leadership in a church, when there are local lay leaders who have proved they can do the job perfectly well themselves.

Deacons

The ministry of deacons was clearly regarded as a separate ministry from that of elders, for in 1 Timothy they are distinguished from one another and treated separately. There are some who would trace their origin to Acts 6. If so, it is rather strange to find such "deacons" performing miracles and preaching publicly (Acts 6:8), and one of them acting as a healer and evangelist (Acts 8:5-8), and baptising his converts (Acts 8:12)! Some have sought the origin of deacons in the *ḥazzan* or attendant at the synagogues. But this is unlikely, as when this person is mentioned in the New Testament he is not called a *diakonos* but *huperetes* (Luke 4:20). It is, however, almost certain that the order of deacons has no parallel in Jewish or Gentile institutions. If so, it is interesting to reflect that, while the early Christians were perfectly happy to carry over an institution like the presbyterate from Judaism, they were equally prepared to break new ground with the setting up of a diaconate without precedent at the time. Leon Morris has written, 'Under the leadership of the Holy Spirit of God they could and did walk in the old paths or strike out into the new, according as the need arose. Flexibility is the characteristic of the attitude of the early Church, a characteristic which has not always remained in later generations.'[13] It would be nice to think that the one really original office invented by the early Christians was the diaconate; if so, it has it own significance, for the element of service is the overriding consideration for all ministry in the New Testament.

It would seem clear that the ministry of deacons and their female equivalent deaconesses (there is no feminine gender for the Greek word *diakonos*), is an auxiliary one in the New Testament. It was a kind of back-up ministry for the leaders of the Church, setting them free from administrative chores so that they could concentrate on the exacting task of pastoring the people of God. Even if the happenings in Acts 6 are not a description of the origin of the order of deacons, they do demonstrate the reasonableness of having people to "serve tables", and thus release the leadership of the Church to do its work properly. At all events, the result of this setting free of the apostles was growth, for, 'the word of God increased and the number of the disciples multiplied greatly in Jerusalem' (Acts 6:7). As we have seen, it is likely that the deacons mentioned in Philippians 1:1 were the trustees of the money which had been raised by the Philippian Church. It is easy to see the role of the deacons in the early Church, as the administrators and businessmen of the Church, concerned more with things than people, but looking after the material needs of the brethren (such as the Hellenistic widows in Acts 6). There is little doubt that by the second century the so-called three-fold ministry of bishops, presbyters and deacons had become the rule for most of the Christian Church.

I have argued elsewhere against the retention of the diaconate as it is at present conceived in Anglican and

Roman Catholic tradition. The diaconate in the New Testament is not a leadership ministry. It is there to serve the leadership (just as the leadership is there to serve the diaconate), and both have quite distinctive functions, although both need their own charism if they are to be able to function effectively. In a sense, the whole of the Church is a diaconate. Nevertheless, there will always be a need for administrators and helpers in the Church, and it is important that they are seen as possessing no less a calling and an anointing from God than the presbyterate.

But it would be a great pity if the revival of the diaconate were regarded as another rank in the professional army of Christ. We have already noticed the baneful effect of professionalism in the Church. If the Church is to have deacons, and all churches do need faithful and honest administrators, let them all be laymen, but properly recognised. Some, in large church situations, may need to be full-time. Most will earn their own living. But that is not the point. The real issue concerns ordination. Suffice it to say that ordination, as we at present understand it, is for leadership and, therefore, it should not be given to deacons. Instead of ordination it should be a simple matter of recognising the needs in each local situation and appointing for the tasks in hand the persons who will have the appropriate gifts for the work that is to be undertaken.

As for other ministries in the local church, we should look for and expect the Holy Spirit to provide everything that is needful, including 'teachers, workers of miracles, healers, helpers, administrators, speakers in various kinds of tongues' (1 Cor. 12:28). But we have concentrated in this chapter on the ministry of leadership in the local church. In the next we need to turn our attention to the rather more controversial area of ministry in the wider and universal Church.

12

Are Bishops Really Necessary?

If we are fairly sure of our ground when writing about leadership in the local church, we move into a veritable minefield when we look at leadership outside the local scene. Here we immediately run up against controversy, for we come face to face with denominational structures amongst Protestants, and with the hierarchical institutions of the Roman Catholic Church. And even if we have gone for a new, simple pattern of independency, such as a "house church", we can't enjoy that luxury for very long before we have to begin thinking hard what our relationship and commitment should be to the rest of the Church. Before we know where we are we can be involved in a new denominational structure based on a new set of agreements. It may at first only look like a fresh alignment, but all too quickly it jells into a federation of churches, and, therefore, a denomination. But we know we cannot shirk the difficult task, for we dare not isolate ourselves from other churches, any more than we can live as Christians on our own.

We are not primarily concerned in this book with the Church as such, but with ministry in the Church. And when we go outside the local church, if we are going to be realistic we are bound to have a good hard look at episcopacy. Even if we regard bishops as superfluous, we cannot ignore the facts that from earliest times until the Reformation episcopacy dominated the Church, and that many of the Reformers accepted episcopacy also. At the present time no one can possibly take ecumenism seriously without at the same time taking episcopacy seriously. It is inconceivable that any future united Church, which included Churches with episcopal church government, would not have bishops. And if one's vision for future unity includes the Roman Catholic Church, then a non-episcopal church government would be completely out of the question. If we are to think seriously about leadership beyond the local church, we must at least begin by looking at episcopacy.

When we turn to the New Testament we are immediately confronted with a problem. Bishops are not there. The word *episcopos* is used, but it is clearly a synonym for the much more frequently used word *presbuteros*. The office of bishop as we now understand it, and, indeed, as church history at least since the beginning of the second century has recognised it, was unknown to the early Church. We shall see later that there were probably models, but we cannot even be sure of that. On the other hand the office of apostle is clearly designated; yet by the second century apostles had ceased. Somewhere in the immediate post-apostolic period the Church did a switch from apostolic to episcopal government, and there is still today considerable controversy as to how, when, and why this happened. There are a number of ingenious suggestions, but, for the moment, we are only concerned with stating the fact, about which there is no controversy, that in the second century, first in the East but then spreading to the Western part of the Church, episcopacy became the generally recognised form of supra-local government.

Since those early days, episcopacy has had a very varied history. We cannot go into all the vicissitudes it has passed through. But it is still the only accepted form of supra-local church government for most of the Christian Church, and has even been accepted by some Pentecostal Churches in the twentieth century. One gets the feeling today that if one didn't have bishops one would have to invent them. But whether we call them bishops or not, the need for some kind of ministry and church government which is larger than the local church is accepted by most Churches in Christendom today. So, whilst we shall be mainly concerned with episcopacy as such, those who do not accept this title of leadership can quite well substitute their own, for our main concern is with Christian leadership which is wider in scope than that of the local church.

Apostles in the New Testament

We must begin with the New Testament, and, therefore, we need to look closely at the apostles, and, since in some key passages they are linked together, with the prophets. It is interesting to notice how often in the New Testament the very words used on some occasions to designate a particular ministry or office are on other occasions used to describe a general ministry in which the whole Body of Christ is involved. We have already seen that this is true of the word *diakonos*. It is equally true of the word *episkopos*. This has been pointed out by John Stott in an address given at the Islington Clerical Conference in 1966.[1] He showed how in Hebrews 12:15 ('see to it that no one fails to obtain the grace of God'), the words "see to it" translate the Greek word *episkopountes*. They are a general exhortation to members of the local church to accept spiritual responsibility for each other. Moulton and Milligan quote papyrus examples of the use of the verb as a common salutation at the end of letters. So we can say, according to strict New Testament word usage, that every bishop is a presbyter and that every believer is a bishop. The same may be said in a more general sense of the word *apostellō*. In Acts 8 it was the "laity" who became "apostolic", when there was a persecution against the Church in Jerusalem, and the apostles who stayed at home to face the music. In Vatican II Cardinal Lercaro, in a debate on *charisma*, said, 'Every Catholic must be an apostle. His apostolate is performed by prayer, example and preaching.'[2] All this would indicate that the early Christians did not have in their thinking a yawning gap between some who held an exalted position in the Church and the *hoi poloi* or inferior. Ministry was a partnership between all the members of the Body of Christ, and in fact 'God has so adjusted the body' that he gives 'the greater honour to the inferior part that there may be no discord in the body, but that the members may have the same care for one another' (1 Cor. 12:24-5). Eduard Schweizer and Ernst Käsemann have in their writings emphasised the dynamic concept of authority and ministry in the New Testament compared with the traditional static one. Schweizer writes, 'With Paul charism and ministry are both regarded essentially as an event, as something that takes place',[3] and Käsemann, 'The apostle's theory of order is not a static one, resting on offices, institutions, ranks and dignities; in his view, authority resides only within the concrete act of ministry as it occurs.'[4] Hans Küng's emphasis on the continuing charismatic structure of the Church points in the same direction.[5] But, having said all that needs to be said about the general episcopal and apostolic nature of the Church and its ministry, we still need to recognise and, therefore, look carefully at the place of distinctive ministries or offices in the Church, both in New Testament times and today.

It is obvious that in the New Testament the word "apostle" is used in a variety of ways, again demonstrating the un-fussy nature of the New Testament writers' approach to ministry. Even such a high and honourable word as "apostle" is used to describe comparatively humble ministry. Thus in 2 Corinthians 8:23 and Philippians 2:25 (and possibly Romans 16:7) the word is used to describe messengers. Vincent Taylor has distinguished between four groups of apostles in the New Testament. First were the Jerusalem apostles (the Twelve, and James the brother of Jesus);- second, the apostles of Antioch (Paul, Barnabas and Silas), who supervised the Gentile churches. Then there were apostles with local assignments among the Gentiles (for example, Andronicus

and Junias, Rom. 16:7). Finally there were those who
performed apostolic ministries without being expressly called
"apostle" in the New Testament, such as Timothy and Titus.[6]
James Dunn distinguishes in a simpler fashion, in describing
Paul's use of the word, between the apostles who are, in a
sense, representatives of another person's authority and those
who have an authority over the local church (as in 1 Cor.
12:28). He sees Paul as typical of the second of these. Such
men had been personally commissioned by Christ in a
resurrection appearance. They were involved in founding
churches, and they had a distinctively and decisively eschatological role.[7] R. Bultmann simplifies the matter still further.
'Paul calls all missionaries "apostles",' he writes.[8] But this
would be to widen the use of the word too much.

What does seem to emerge from the New Testament is
that, while the word "apostle" is used to describe people who
are sent on a mission by someone else, thus conforming to the
popular use of the word in contemporary Judaism, its
primary use is to describe a very small band of men with a
particular (and I would say *unique*) role. This would include
the Twelve (less Judas Iscariot, plus Matthias), the apostle
Paul, and James, the brother of Jesus. The uniqueness of
their ministry and its unrepeatable nature lay in two areas.
First, they were the founders of the Christian Church.
Secondly, some were the men whom Christ chose to be the
main contributors to the New Testament. In these two
respects they were called to do something which, because of
its very nature, could not be repeated.

Paul indicates this unique role in Ephesians 2:19-21, when
he talks of the Church as the 'household of God, built upon
the foundation of the apostles and prophets, Christ Jesus
himself being the cornerstone, in whom the whole structure is
joined together and grows into a holy temple in the Lord'.
One obvious thing about a foundation is that it is only laid
once. It would also seem to be indicated by the words of Jesus
to Peter in Matthew 16:19, 'I will give you the keys of the
Kingdom of Heaven.' Peter had a unique role in opening the

Jewish world to the gospel at Pentecost, the Samaritan world (with John) as recorded in Acts 8, and the Gentile world in the house of the centurion Cornelius at Caesarea (Acts 10). They are doors which, once opened, have never needed to be opened again. Of course, there have been many church planters ever since, and pioneer missionaries like Columba, Patrick, Francis Xavier, Hudson Taylor, who have opened up countries to the gospel. But they have been building on the foundation laid by the apostles and prophets and the cornerstone of Christ, in whom the whole structure is joined together. As James Dunn points out, the *particular* sense in which Paul exercised his apostolic ministry was as founder of a specific community. 'Apostles, in Paul's view at least, were no figures commanding authority in any and every church; their authority was limited to their sphere of operation, to the churches they founded.'[9]

The role of the apostles as the ones chosen to transmit to the Church the teaching of Christ is also clear. In this area we see, too, how important it was that they had actually seen the resurrected Lord. When Matthias was chosen to replace Judas Iscariot, the candidates were chosen from those, who, according to the words of Peter, 'have accompanied us during all the time that the Lord Jesus went in and out among us... One of these men must become with us a witness to his resurrection' (Acts 1:2). Paul, in setting forward his claims to be a true apostle writes, 'Am I not an apostle? Have I not seen Jesus our Lord?' (1 Cor. 9:1). The apostles had this in common, *they had all seen the Lord.* They were in a unique position to transmit to the Church of all future generations the teachings of Christ. Their witness to Jesus was *direct*, while all other witness is *derived*. Paul puts this clearly in Galatians 1:1-12. His reception of the gospel was *di'apokalypseos* (by revelation) not *di'anthrōpou* (through human intermediaries). The second-century Church recognised this role by taking good care only to admit to the canon those writings which they knew emanated from the apostolic circle. We believe today because of their word. Jesus prayed for 'those who believe in me *through their word*' (John 17:20).

It has been argued by some, such as Watchman Nee, that we are to expect "apostles of the Church" today. The argument goes that there is a difference between the apostles of the Lord Jesus Christ (the Twelve), who constituted an unrepeatable ministry, and the apostles of the Church (or of the Holy Spirit), who would have included Paul and others, which is a ministry we should expect today. One of the scriptural sources of this teaching is Ephesians 4:11. So, the argument goes, since the gifts (which include apostles) are given by Christ after his ascension (see verses 7-10), they must refer to people other than the Twelve, for they were appointed *before* Christ's ascension. The argument is at first sight very plausible. But it is distinctly shaky on several grounds. It is surely inconceivable that Paul, in talking about the ministries of the world-wide Church, and in mentioning apostles, would have included himself, but excluded the likes of Peter, James and John. Although it is true that the apostles were *appointed* during Christ's earthly life, yet they did not begin to *function* until after Pentecost, and, as we have often seen, the New Testament is more concerned about function than appointment to the ministry. On these grounds alone the Watchman Nee interpretation should be seriously questioned.

It is best, surely, to see the apostolic office, in the sense of an authoritative ministry in the Church, as being intended only for the early days of the Church. In the secondary sense, as messengers or missionaries, the ministry has continued. Indeed it is an important aspect of the total ministry of the Church, as we have already seen. Likewise, there was clearly a special and unique role for prophets in the early Church, and on into the second century, before the Canon of the New Testament had become established and largely accepted throughout the Christian world. Prophets were often linked with apostles in church founding (see Eph. 2:20) and ministry (see especially Acts 13:1). They too seem to have been itinerants, as well as having at times a settled ministry in the Church. Eduard Schweizer has written, 'From the removal of the Galileans to Jerusalem until the withdrawal to Pella, the way of the Church was essentially determined by the directions of the Spirit through prophets and other members of the Church.'[10] A high place is assigned to prophets in the Didache. There they are called "the high priests of the Church" (13:3). But by the end of the second century the prophets were on the way out. The New Testament canon was nearly established and there was less need for their type of ministry. But it is most important to recognise that, while prophets ceased in the sense of an authoritative ministry similar to that of the apostles, the prophetic element has always remained in the Church, mushrooming up at its better moments, and only being quenched by institutionalism and scribalism, such as extreme fundamentalism. The prophecy of Joel, which saw its fulfil-ment on the day of Pentecost, declares the new age to be one of profuse prophesying: 'I will pour out my Spirit and they shall prophesy' (Acts 2:18). The charismatic gift of prophecy has continued in the Church ever since, as has the ministry of the prophet in a secondary sense like that of apostles. There have been moments in church history when prophesyings have been despised, especially in the more cerebral times. But we should not today be looking for prophets in the sense in which some were regarded in the New Testament, namely as second only to the apostles and vitally involved in those roles which were unrepeatable, the founding of the Church and the establishment of the New Testament scriptures. As far as apostles are concerned, let Schweizer have the last word:[11]

The New Testament is unanimous that the apostle in the narrower sense acquires a unique position because of his meeting with the risen — or exalted — Lord (in whatever different ways that position may be understood), and because of the charge given him. To him (perhaps to others too) there is entrusted the fundamental preaching by which the later preaching is to be measured. We can speak of the apostles' pupils, but not of their successors in office.

To the scriptural evidence needs to be added the unfailing testimony of Church tradition, for there was no attempt after the death of the apostles to perpetuate the apostolate. There are a few references to apostles in literature such as the Didache. But there is a kind of fog between about A.D. 70 and the turn of the century. The Church seems to have suffered from a kind of corporate amnesia. We do not know for sure exactly what happened. There are many theories. But all we do know for sure is that the Church went into the fog with apostles and emerged with bishops! There is a possibility, of course, that some in the Church were guilty of an act of cunning duplicity, like a conjurer producing a rabbit out of a hat or turning a red sheet into a green one. But what is much more likely is that a combination of expediency (which after all is how much ministry in the New Testament developed anyway, owing to the serious exigencies of the time) and the wisdom of the leadership, coupled with the genius of the Holy Spirit, gave birth to episcopacy in the second century, although the conception of the idea does come from the New Testament itself. Certainly the Church in this period had to face a crisis of extraordinary magnitude. Within a few years it was to lose through martyrdom three out of its four most outstanding leaders — Paul, Peter and James, the brother of Jesus. In A.D. 70 Jerusalem was sacked by the Romans, and so the Church lost its centre, to which Christians from many countries had looked for leadership. It had had advantages at that time over any other city, because it had been the place of Christ's death and resurrection, and of the first Pentecost. The Church had to face a leadership crisis of the highest magnitude.

But there was an even more serious problem facing the Church. Gnosticism had been gaining ground for some time. It now threatened to overthrow the whole Church. There have always been those who have thought that Gnostic heresies were the catalyst which precipitated the establishment of episcopacy. Jerome himself said that episcopacy was not original but was founded 'to cure schism', and Irenaeus regarded the succession of bishops as a safeguard against Gnostic heretics. It would have been natural, when the Church was threatened in the areas of both its Christian unity and doctrinal purity, and when it had lost its outstanding leaders, for it to have looked for some external authority and focus of unity and so given birth to episcopal leadership, which during the second century became universally accepted throughout the Church. Certainly episcopacy was never seriously challenged by anyone. It became a system of church government which was both to unite and sustain the Church for a long time to come. One cannot but believe that it was the genius of the Holy Spirit which created it.

Episcopacy has had its ups-and-downs ever since. There have been more than a few proud prelates: some scoundrels — even criminals. There have been others who have served the Church indifferently. But at the same time many of the Church's greatest saints and scholars have been bishops.

The Catholic Apostolic Church

Before we go on to examine the origins of episcopacy we need to look at the one serious attempt through these many centuries to restore the ministry of apostles to the universal Church. We refer, of course, to the Catholic Apostolic Church of the nineteenth century.

There has been a spate of new interest in Edward Irving and the Catholic Apostolic Church in the last few years. There have been a few who have seen this nineteenth-century movement as a precursor of the twentieth-century Pentecostal movement.[12] One who has written favourably about the Catholic Apostolic Church is Larry Christenson. In his book, *A Message to the Charismatic Movement*[13] he sees it as bearing 'striking resemblances to the Charismatic Movement'. So we need to look a little closer at this new church which emerged just before Queen Victoria came to the throne, and "died" the same year as that august monarch did — 1901 — with the passing of the last remaining "apostle".

It was in 1830 that Mary Campbell was miraculously healed and began to speak in tongues in her home in Fernicarry, Scotland. At about the same time Margaret McDonald was healed at the command of her brother James at Port Glasgow. The fact that a Campbell and a MacDonald were the first to receive these experiences has a significance which is not lost on a Scot. For the benefit of the uninitiated, the Campbells 'have no dealings' with the MacDonalds. The news soon reached London, where there was a group of people who had been praying for a recovery of spiritual gifts. The MacDonalds soon dropped out of the picture. They refused to get involved, because they regarded the Irvingites as "unscriptural", but Mary Campbell went to live in London and attended Edward Irving's Church, where on occasions she interrupted Irving's sermons with her gift of tongues. It was Mrs. John Cardale, the wife of a prominent Anglican lawyer, who was the first of the London group to speak in tongues. During 1830-1832 the movement spread in London, and was focused in the public mind on the person of Edward Irving, who was the minister of the National Scottish Church in Regent Square and one of London's foremost preachers.

Edward Irving began to preach in favour of this new movement, and allowed the gifts of the Spirit to be manifested in the regular worship services. When we remember that this was 1830 and not 1970, it is not really surprising that Irving and his strange friends were locked outside the Church; nor can we blame the trustees for this. According to A. L. Drummond, the gifts were manifested in a disorderly fashion, mostly by women, who were not averse to interrupting sermons in voices which were not their own.[14] The possibility that the movement in its initial stages had satanic aspects needs to be taken seriously, not only because of the way in which the gifts were manifested in the services, but also because of information we have about Mary Campbell, who testified amongst other things to automatic letter-writing.

In view of what happened, the Irvingites moved to another building and set up their own church. Edward Irving himself died soon afterwards (in December 1834), and he never took much part in the formation of the Catholic Apostolic Church. Irving is an enigmatic character. There is much to love, much to pity, and much to question. He was undoubtedly guilty of heresy concerning his teaching about Christ's humanity, although it would not cause the slightest ripple in the permissive theological climate of today. He became increasingly anti-intellectual and naïve about gifts. He believed that one should have an attitude of absolute submission to utterances in the Spirit, and that it was wrong to judge them. He developed a blind sectarian spirit that was increasingly anti-Church. The organised Church to him was "Babylon". He was highly imaginative and impetuous by nature. His intensity did not endear him to his contemporaries and colleagues. But there is no doubt that his trial for heresy was a cruel and vindictive affair. Perhaps his greatest deficiency was that he lacked common sense and a sense of humour. If only he could have laughed at himself it might have been another story, for he was without doubt a man of singular ability and one of the greatest orators of his century. As it did in his circle of friends, the Second Coming took a disproportionate place in his interests, and in his commentary on the book of Daniel he is not afraid to mention dates. Right at the end of his life, according to A. L. Drummond, he recanted of his convictions, although Henry Drummond, one of the "apostles" tried to destroy the evidence. But one should not base too much on this. Irving was by then a very sick man, and had suffered much both from his charismatic friends and from the Church of Scotland.

But Edward Irving was never an "apostle". From as early as 1830 there had been prayer meetings in Port Glasgow when the words were spoken, 'Send us *apostles,* send *apostles, apostles,* to prepare the Bride.' It was this cry which became

the obsession of the movement. The Irvingites believed they
had been called to set up a kind of prototype and pure
Church on earth to prepare the way for the coming of Christ.
This was to be the last Church, and they believed that the
rest of the Church — Roman Catholic, Eastern Orthodox
and Protestant — was to swing into line with them. The key
was the setting up of the apostles. They believed that the
Christian Church had committed a serious blunder by
withdrawing the apostles at the end of the first century. They
argued that apostles are so important and fundamental to the
life of the Church that to remove them was disastrous. 'The
punishment was the postponement of the Lord's return, and
the loss of the apostolic office.'[15] Their logic was obvious.
Restore the apostles, and the bridegroom will come. So they
restored the apostles, *but the Bridegroom didn't come*. They made
no provision for the appointing of any further apostles, for the
simple reason that they were certain there would be no need.
They would experience the Lord's Return, for at last the
Church was returning to its position of obedience. The
apostles were back, and so the Lord would be back quite
soon.

It would seem that only two conclusions can possibly be
reached about the Catholic Apostolic Church: it was either
naïve or pretentious. Since the leaders were all highly
intelligent people, it would be difficult to apply the epithet
"naïve". Self-deceived perhaps, but not naïve. Here I must
differ from Larry Christenson's conclusions. In fact, the
Catholic Apostolic Church seems to have contained many of
the worst features of a charismatic movement. It is a warning
to the charismatic movement of today and it needs to be
taken seriously. Although the Irvingites often claimed that
they were 'a Church within the Church' and denied that they
were sectarian, nevertheless they did set up a new denomination, with separate ministries, sacraments and churches in
different parts of the world. They were never a renewal
movement within the disciplines of the historic churches.
They were also from the start an exclusive fellowship. The

"apostles" were all members of the landed gentry, rich, self-sufficient and socially "upper class". Their churches were always in the wealthy parts of the country, to match the social standing of the leadership. Although they were supposed to be preparing the world-wide Church for Christ's return, they sent out no missionaries, had little or no concern for evangelism, and their churches are only to be found in the rich countries of the West.

Their most baneful legacy to the churches is in the area of eschatology. They were obsessed with this subject, as were many of their contemporaries, particularly the equally schismatic Plymouth Brethren, who were developing at about the same time. Although the pre-millennial view of Christ's return can be traced back to early Patristic sources, nevertheless it owes much to the Catholic Apostolic Church for its recovery to favour in the Western Protestant world, and it was soon to become, with most unfortunate side-effects, the dominant eschatology of the famous 'Bible Belt' of America. Henry Drummond, one of the "apostles", was particularly neurotic about the Second Coming. In 1836 he went off to inform the Archbishop of York that the end of the world was imminent. He went on doing this all through his life. In 1860 he invited Thomas Carlyle and his wife to Albury Court to await the Lord's Return. A few months later Drummond was dead. Carlyle wrote about this in his diary. 'In a few months more Henry himself was dead; and no more mistakes possible again.'

The movement had a sad ending. Cardale, the first and in many ways chief "apostle", admitted that their expectation of the Lord's return had been mistaken. Their pretentiousness is seen in their belief that they were God's élite, chosen before all others to head up God's end-time Church and bring in the Millennium. It was only later that they adjusted their views and saw themselves as a "John the Baptist" movement to prepare the way for another charismatic movement. When this began to happen at the turn of the century with the birth of the Pentecostal Movement they did not grasp its significance. It is a warning to some modern charismatics who are attempting again to restore the apostolic office.

The only other real attempt to restore the apostolate was made by one of the Pentecostal Churches in Britain, which originated in Wales following the revival at the beginning of the twentieth century. They called themselves the Apostolic Church, and their headquarters is still in Penygroes in South Wales. They have churches in other parts of Britain and the world, and are keenly evangelistic, in marked contrast to the Catholic Apostolic Church. But their influence even amongst Pentecostals has not been very great.[16]

Origins of episcopacy

If the Christians at the end of the first century were crying 'Send us apostles', the Lord seems to have answered by sending them bishops! We must now address ourselves to the question of the origins of episcopacy and its place in the Church today.

There are those who have argued for the so-called Apostolic Succession, that is to say that there has been an unbroken succession of bishops going back to Peter himself. The major difficulty with this theory is the hidden period we have already mentioned between A.D. 70 and the first clear mention of episcopacy as we know it today by Ignatius at the beginning of the second century. Any attempt to say what happened in that period is bound to be somewhat speculative. According to Rothe's ingenious reconstruction the one remaining "chief" apostle, John, was largely responsible for establishing episcopacy in those traumatic years following the deaths of Peter, Paul and James and the overthrow of Jerusalem. This view is rebutted by Eduard Schweizer, who sees the Johannine Epistles as a protest against the threat of a monarchical episcopate.[17] But there is not time to discuss this fascinating question; all we do know for certain is that episcopacy appeared at the beginning of the second century and had taken the place of the apostolate, and that it spread inexorably throughout the Church and was never seriously challenged at that time. Its hold over the Church was to continue virtually until the Reformation.

But it is important to notice that although the word "bishop" is another name for "elder" in the New Testament, it certainly is not a synonym for "apostle". The two offices were distinctly different. The apostles' role was largely to travel and to found churches, over which they exercised strong pastoral oversight. Moreover, their authority, as we have seen, derived very directly from Christ himself. Bishops also travelled, but over a much smaller area. They were not primarily concerned with starting new churches, but with exercising pastoral care over existing ones and uniting them together. Their authority was similar to that of elders, only over a number of churches rather than over people within one church. Oscar Cullmann says, 'The function of the bishop, which is transmitted, is essentially different from that of the apostle, which cannot be transmitted... The bishops succeed the apostles but on a completely different level. They succeed them not as apostles but as bishops, whose office is also important for the church, but quite distinct.'[18] In another book, he makes the famous statement, 'The apostolate does not belong to the period of the Church, but to that of the Incarnation of Christ.'[19] In the same book he very interestingly draws attention to the fact that the apostles become the norm of doctrine in the early Church (Acts 2:42), and thus the New Testament attributes the same images to Jesus as the apostles — for example "rocks" and the corresponding images of "foundation", "pillars". *But these are never used to designate the bishop.* The danger facing the Church at the end of the first century was that the gospel would fall to pieces in the face of gnostic intellectualism, and become something timeless and unhistorical. The origins of episcopacy derive, almost certainly, from the urgent task of holding together the Church and bringing it into unity on the foundation of apostolic doctrine. Perhaps one of the most perspicacious statements on this comes from Bishop Lightfoot. 'The episcopate was formed not out of the apostolic order by localisation but out of the presbyteral by elevation, and the title, which originally was common to all, came at length to be appropriated to the chief among them.'[20] Or to put it another way, bishops are but presbyters "writ large". They were originally *primus inter pares*. Their role was to be shepherds to the shepherds, amongst whom they lived and worked, and to whose spiritual welfare they were chiefly dedicated. They 'came up from the ranks'. They were never an authority imposed from above or outside. Their exceptional gifts clearly indicated that their ministry lay with a wider fellowship than with a local church. As the *pastor pastorum*, the bishop held the Church together, and guided it over the questions which arose concerning faith, order and morals. The bishops were the outstanding leaders amongst the leaders, who had proved themselves beyond any shadow of doubt to be worthy of the position they held. It was supremely pastoral concern that led to the creation of the episcopate. But it was not some "new thing". It was essentially a part of the general presbyterate, only instead of having oversight over a local church, the episcopate had oversight over the elders, and was a focus of unity of the whole Church rather than the local church.

There are some who have seen the model of what later became monarchical episcopacy in the fascinating ministry of James, the brother of Jesus. He is called an apostle by Paul in Galatians 1:19, and obviously held an important position of influence in the early formative years of the Church. When referring, for example, to the pillars of the Church, Paul mentions James before Peter and John (Gal. 2:9). Even more significant is the fact that in Acts 15, at the so-called council of Jerusalem, it is James who presides, does a summary of the discussions and suggests a decision. Again in Acts 21 it is James who receives Paul (v. 18). The obvious difference between James and the other apostles is that he didn't travel as they did. He was not a founder of churches. Instead he was the "overseer" of the headquarters Church in Jerusalem, which was clearly very large and influential. So it is not surprising that some see him as exercising a ministry similar to that of a later diocesan bishop. There are several who very early on regarded him as the first bishop of Jerusalem, namely Eusebius, Epiphanius, Chrysostom and Jerome. The Pseudo-Clementines also indicate that he was a most impressive leader. But what is more interesting, in view of the emergence of a more despotic episcopate in the second century, is that James does seem to have shared his leadership with the elders of the Church in Jerusalem, and this is particularly evident at the council described in Acts 15. Paul and Barnabas went up to Jerusalem, we are told, 'to the apostles *and the elders*' (verse 2), who are again linked together in verse 4. In verse 6 the gathering is described as 'the apostles and the elders', with James clearly in the chair. We see here the important principle of plurality or collegiality of leadership. Thus later on the bishop comes from the "college" of elders, and is their president or chairman. Thus those who have authority in the Church are not imposed on the Church from some even higher authority, but are raised up within the Church by common consent and approbation.

Bishops today

It is a far cry from the days of Ignatius, who wrote to the Church in Ephesus, on his way to martyrdom in Rome, 'We ought to regard the Bishop as the Lord Himself.' When someone accidentally prayed in the Litany for the "elimination" of all Bishops, he may well have been expressing the views of some. But they certainly need "illumination", as the whole Church does with regard to their future. In 1918 Charles Gore wrote to William Temple, 'Episcopacy is only carrying on.' In 1944 William Temple died tragically of gout only two years after becoming Archbishop of Canterbury. As everyone acknowledges it was work that killed him. Writing in the *Spectator*, shortly after his death, the Bishop of Southwell grimly commented, 'Is the Church so rich in prophets that it can afford to squander the gifts of God?' F. A. Iremonger, who wrote Archbishop Temple's biography, recalls in it his last talk with him:[21]

As I looked across the hearthrug at that spent man with the tired eyes and ill-regulated engagement-book, whom Christians of every name were trusting for leadership and inspiration in the post-war years, I could only ask with shame and amazement Dr. Barry's question, 'Is the Church so rich in prophets that it can afford to squander the gifts of God?'

Dr. Barry in the same article in the *Spectator* pleaded, 'Some re-arrangement has become imperative.' In the years that have followed little re-arrangement has taken place, and the strains of episcopal office have taken several others to a premature grave, and converted others into virtual zombies. It is not unheard of for some, in their tiredness and loneliness, to take to the bottle. The fact that the majority seem to survive and carry on is to their endless credit, but shame to the Church, which continues to heap burdens upon them as if they had limitless resources of time and energy. If as a result of all this bishops become yes-men and safe conformists, who dare accuse them of betraying their high calling? Some re-arrangement is urgently needed, for we are facing the possibilities of serious losses in leadership, not only because of the strain put on existing leaders, but also because of the temptation many have to turn down such leadership when they see their own gifts being put to better use in other ways. The increasingly administrative role of bishops suits the job specifications of a layman rather than of a man called to spiritual leadership and oversight in the Church.

If we are here particularly referring to episcopacy, the same remarks may equally well apply to the other forms of leadership adopted by other denominations — such as Methodist chairmen and superintendents or Presbyterian moderators. The main complaint which has rightly been levelled at the modern practice of episcopacy is that it has ceased to have any real *pastoral* significance, and it does not seem to arise from the grass roots, or even to have any obvious association with them. It just does not make pastoral sense. As Colin Buchanan has written:[22]

To isolate episcopacy as something which can, so to speak, be injected into a Church without organic relation to its faith, liturgical practice, and pastoral structure is not only to reduce episcopacy to 'gimmick' or mascot status, it is to empty it of its historic meaning and to invert its real purpose. Episcopacy is not an accolade bestowed on the Church as a finishing touch or a final decoration, nor is it a trifle of which a Church should make as little as possible, lest its members be offended. The historic episcopate — which, as such, must be sharply distinguished from the corrupt prelatical forms it has too often taken — *is a pattern of apostolic pastoral ministry.* (Italics mine)

The bishop is, alas, hardly a "pattern of pastoral ministry" today. With large dioceses it is virtually impossible for a modern bishop to fulfil his proper pastoral function, nor can he with any stretch of the imagination exercise collegial leadership *amongst* his fellow elders or fellow bishops. The plain truth of the matter, as many people have pointed out, is that there are too few bishops. John Stott has rightly said that either the unit or diocese needs 'to be small enough, or its overseers must be numerous enough for this personal relationship to exist between sheep and shepherd. There may well be biblical warrant for more bishops and smaller dioceses... otherwise all the flock will not be tended; some will be neglected, even forgotten.'[23] The Church has never really come to terms *pastorally* with the population explosion; to create a few assistant or suffragan bishops is not enough. The Church will not grow or mature unless there is adequate pastoral care being exercised both in the local church and in the universal Church.

We shall be dealing in the next chapter with the qualifications for leadership in the Church. But what should normally happen is that the gifted leadership comes gradually to the top of the pile. Thus in the local church, the elders are conspicuous because they possess the necessary gifts for their role. As elders come to their positions of leadership, so amongst the elders will be those who have gifts which ought to be made available to the wider Church. These are the people who should be elevated to the episcopate. The five-fold ministry mentioned by Paul in Ephesians 4 should normally be seen in the group of elders who lead a local church. Few people will be, as individuals, proficient in all five areas of ministry. But the more gifted leaders will usually have not only a balanced understanding of these five areas, but also a general aptitude in most and a brilliance in some. Thus bishops should be prophetic in their understanding of the Church and the world, able to understand how God sees things and to see into the future, so that the Church does not lag behind but is always up-to-date and relevant. They need pastoral gifts, and the ability to handle people. They should be able to teach and to grasp the wholeness of Christian doctrine, so that they can uphold the truth and refute error and false teaching. They should have charismatic abilities, and be leaders in evangelism. No one person can be outstanding in all these areas; but, provided the principle of collegiality is adopted, others can fill in where there are weaknesses.

The image of bishops today is often a false one. They are represented by the media as "establishment" figures, and one cannot help feeling that some like it that way. They are thought of as "safe" and defenders of the *status quo*. They are far from being regarded as charismatic in the right sense of that word. The reaction of many bishops and other church leaders to the charismatic movement has been typically guarded, as if they are not sure how to handle it. But they ought to be the leaders of charismatic Christianity. There have been times when they were. They performed "the signs of an apostle", and were thought to be all the better qualified because of this. Bishops have been great evangelists and sometimes healers. In Sydney, Australia, in 1975, the Bishop of Singapore was challenged by the Press because of his ministry of healing — as if this was something that bishops just don't possess. The Bishop, however, opened his prayer book and showed a rather startled reporter the words that the archbishop says to a new bishop at his consecration — 'Hold up the weak, *heal the sick*, bind up the broken, bring again the outcasts, seek the lost' — a clear exhortation to bishops to practise evangelism and divine healing. Would to God all bishops did this! How transforming it could be if confirmation services were evangelistic in the sense that people were challenged by the bishop to come to Christ, and if bishops prayed, not only for the candidates, but also for any others present to be filled with the Holy Spirit, and if the bishop prayed for the sick and ministered deliverance to people with mental and emotional problems. This could well be done by the bishop and a team of elders and others who are gifted in these areas. Bishops should be giving adventurous leadership, and expecting God to work in all these areas of human need when they visit local churches. They should be helping to co-ordinate and promote the mission of the Church to the world, and the continuous renewal of the Church's life in the power of the Holy Spirit. They should also be gifted with discernment, and be able to help others distinguish between the real and the counterfeit. This is exactly what the second-century bishops did superbly and, when functioning properly, have continued to do so ever since. Thus Ignatius wrote to his fellow bishop Polycarp, 'I exhort you, press on in your course and exhort all men that they may be saved.'[24] It may also surprise some that Irenaeus, for all his deep theological concern, was, according to Michael Green, 'most at home as an evangelist'.[25] He even learned several foreign languages in order to preach the gospel to barbarians.

The modern bishop tends to be a lonely person, and that is good neither for him nor for the Church. The natural tendency is for him to become more and more removed from the local church situation; he therefore cannot really know what is going on, and is tempted to live more and more in a world of fantasy. To protect his position as bishop he has less and less to do with the day-to-day running of the local church, and his contacts with his fellow ministers get more and more casual and remote. It is only when things go wrong or when there is pressing need that he has close fellowship with them. Most diocesan bishops have their own private chapels, and their daily devotional life revolves around them. Apart from a wife, if he has one, and possibly a chaplain, the bishop has few really close relationships. It would be much healthier if bishops were attached to a local church, which they could attend regularly. The local church could undertake to have a special pastoral responsibility for the bishop, and the bishop himself would be able to draw freely and regularly from the life of the community. It would keep him earthed to reality, and help him to understand the pastoral and evangelistic needs of the Church. If there was a regular staff meeting, the bishop would seek to attend it whenever possible. He would be an emeritus member of staff, offering advice and receiving the ministry of encouragement from the community. He would, therefore, be in a "collegial" atmosphere, and he should seek to be "amongst" his fellow elders as often as possible. He need never then be lonely.

It may well be argued that no bishop could possibly find time to belong to a parish church, and that he really belongs to the diocese and should not, therefore, be personally associated with any one parish. It is a reasonable enough argument, but it tends to forget that bishops are human, and that it is quite impossible for one man to give himself to a vast number of churches and people, only a few of whom he is likely to know at all well, and most of whom he is only going to associate with in the most casual of fashions. Is it really necessary that the bishop should be seen everywhere? Is not the bishop's own spiritual life of greater importance, for if that goes stale or awry, then everything will be in vain? No Christian can survive for long, under normal circumstances, or remain sober and balanced, if he is not a part of a community which is large enough to sustain him, and yet small enough for him to have close and warm relationships with others. If a bishop cannot make a local church his "family", then he should develop his own community or support group, with whom he can share his life. [26]

Theologians

Although theologians are not technically leaders, unless they happen to be elders or bishops as well, it is important to examine their role in the Church at large, for obviously their ministry and influence are much wider than the local church they may happen to belong to. In our extremely cerebral form of Christianity in the West there is a tendency to elevate the theologian, and for him, like the bishop, to become more and more detached from the local scene. Dwelling in his own ivory tower, and surveying the scene from afar, he seems to many in the churches to be irrelevant to them. They cannot understand what he is on about, and he is impatient with what he senses to be obscurantism amongst the local leaders of the churches. They tend to be mutually suspicious of one another, and drift further and further apart.

Now, this ought not to be, and needs to be tackled resolutely. First, it ought to be said that a degree in theology does not in and of itself qualify a person to be ordained or to become a church leader locally or trans-locally; nor, we have to add, does it disqualify him! As we shall see in the next chapter, we need to look for certain gifts of leadership, irrespective of theological qualifications. The practice of ordaining people solely or principally on these grounds is most unfortunate. In the Orthodox Churches theologians remain unordained or lay people, and this might be a happy arrangement for those theologians who do not have gifts of leadership along with their intellectual gifts.

But secondly we need to insist, as we have done for bishops, that theologians, whether ordained or lay, belong to local congregations and become committed members of the Church community, and, if possible, involved in the daily life of that community. Without such a commitment the spiritual life of a theologian will deteriorate rapidly, *and so will his theological contribution*, however erudite it may still appear. For theology and experience belong together. For example on the day of Pentecost Peter gave a theological explanation of an *event* of great significance. Something had happened. But many theologians today have little to explain because little is happening, since they are remote from the scene of action. There is a great need for the theologians of the Church to live in a community of faith and love. Theology is itself a charism of the Holy Spirit, and as with every other charism the person who receives it needs to be in a living Christian community if it is to be tested and evaluated properly. It should be a matter of serious concern that some theologians are almost completely isolated from the main stream of Christian life. One wonders if we can really take their theology seriously, when it is so unrelated to the normal life of the Church.

Itinerant ministries

The Church, because it is "apostolic" has raised up itinerant ministries other than apostles, with often unusual and even at times bizarre results. The stronger the local church becomes, the less need there is for such itinerant ministries, and, indeed, there can sometimes be quite violent clashes between the local and the travelling ministries. We see this for example in 3 John 5-8. John praises these travelling ministries and pleads that they should be supported. But apparently there was a man called Diotrephes who had a very different attitude, and refused to welcome these people and actually obstructed others who were welcoming them, and tried to excommunicate them. Obviously he regarded them as a nuisance.

But although itinerant ministries can be a menace when local church life is strong, they come into their own when the local church is weak, for they can often supply what is lacking; they can be a voice crying in a wilderness, and be used to bring renewal to that church. There were many such ministries in the early Church, and they were recognised as part of God's provision for his people. Nevertheless, there had to be safeguards. Not only were there false apostles around, but also there were false teachers, shepherds and prophets, and from earliest times the apostles had to warn the churches to exercise discernment concerning these travellers. Paul talks in 2 Corinthians about "letters of recommendation" (3:1) — the credentials which these men had to carry and show to each church before they were free to minister in them; they were like the officials of gas and electricity companies, who have to carry their credentials and show them before they can be admitted to private houses. Paul warned the Ephesian elders about the "fierce wolves" who would come into the church after his departure "not sparing the flock" (Acts 20:29). The Didache has some interesting rules about how to deal with itinerant preachers and prophets. If they stayed more than two days they were false. They were also deemed false if they asked for money. Here are two tests which, if applied today, would have interesting results.

We are living at a time when the itinerant ministry has come into its own again. There are two main reasons for this. In the first place local churches, and indeed the Church in general, are very weak, and, therefore, in dire need of a blood transfusion from another source. The second reason is that we are living in the jet age which has opened up the world and made travel extraordinarily quick and inexpensive. In the autumn of 1965 three Boeing jets arrived at London Airport crammed with over 400 American business executives. They came to witness for Christ, and travelled throughout Britain for the next two weeks. Such an itinerant ministry would have been impossible until comparatively recently. But this does call for caution. We need again a system of "letters of recommendation". Some shepherds can be really wolves in disguise. There is a need for careful discernment. But the Church at large needs to take this kind of ministry much more seriously. Few Churches have any provision for them. We are still largely bound by the outlook of many years ago, when travel was hard and dangerous, and when very few attempted it. The Church of England, for example, has no real provision for licensing such ministries.

Yet there are real dangers in these ministries. In the first place, the New Testament pattern needs to be followed as far as possible, by which a person always had a travelling companion with him. Secondly, lone ministries are nearly always suspect. A loner is usually a lone wolf. Every travelling ministry needs to be sent from, as far as possible, a local church, and the person who travels needs to be in submission to several others, ideally in a local church, who can vouch for his character and authenticity. One cannot be too careful, and no one should be accepted and invited to minister unless there is clear evidence that he is a *bona fide* Christian who comes from a supportive fellowship of which he is himself a submissive member.

The universal pastor?

In 1975 Pastor Roger Schutz, the Prior of Taizé, went to Rome for an unusual reason. 'I went,' he said, 'to ask pardon of the "universal pastor", Pope Paul VI, for the slowness with which reconciliation is being achieved amongst Christians.' The Prior, who is a Protestant, gave the Pope a fascinating title — "universal pastor". A growing number of Protestant leaders and theologians, while not accepting some of the more extreme notions of the Papal office, are perfectly happy to see the Pope as the chairman of the bishops of the world-wide Church — "the universal pastor", in other words. Who knows, some of us may be alive to see the day of such an acclamation.

13

Who are the Leaders?

UNTIL COMPARATIVELY RECENTLY the necessity of leadership in the Church would not have been seriously questioned by anyone. It has been assumed by most that every kind of society, sacred or secular, has to have clearly designated leadership if it is not going to disintegrate. But today leadership of every kind is under attack. This is partly due to a change in thinking on the part of people and a revolt against authoritative structuring in society and in the home, a desire for freedom from any or most forms of interference, and partly due to the sad fact of corruption in high places and the advantage taken by so many in recent years to use their position of power to tyrannise over people. At the same time, for various reasons, people have been much more ready to be led than to lead, because of the fearful problems of life today and, as a result, there has been a dearth of good leadership in many areas of society. People seem especially loath to shoulder the responsibilities and disciplines which come with leadership of any kind.

On the other hand there has been at least one good thing which has come out of this new situation. We are seeing, in both Church and State, the almost universal acceptance of the principles of power-sharing, and the common understanding of team leadership or, as we have called it elsewhere, the principle of the plurality of eldership. In Britain, the Prime

Minister is more than ever a member of a team, and the country is really governed from the cabinet room rather than from the Prime Minister's office. The sharing of leadership is crucial in the Church also. The danger of monarchical episcopacy is obvious, and in the past bishops have often been little popes. But one would not want to see them little puppets, either. The principle of collegiality, which was one of the most influential shifts of emphasis at Vatican II, can safeguard episcopacy or any other form of Christian leadership from becoming a dictatorship.

If every society needs leadership, and leadership needs to be in the hands of a team, then every team requires a captain. There need be no departure here from the principles already mentioned, for such a leader is always *primus inter pares*. We also should recognise that leadership needs to be strong enough and varied enough to cope with the pastoral needs of the community which it is serving. It is to be remembered that the leaders we are talking about are not "the ministry" of the Church. The whole Church ought to be mobilised for the multifarious tasks and needs it has. The leader's task is to co-ordinate, lead, inspire and train others in the ministry of every church. He is not meant primarily to do the work himself, but to help others to discover their gifts and to develop them fully and for the good of all. Leadership is not a form of domination. According to Hans Küng, 'Its task is to stimulate, co-ordinate and integrate; it serves the communities and the other ministries'.[1] Leaders do not have to be experts in everything. They can always seek expert advice, if necessary, from others. Hans Küng goes on to plead that leadership should not be 'a rigid and uniform system of offices...but flexible, mobile, and pluriform according to time and space... We require pluriform communities, which make a pluriform leadership necessary.'[2] Leaders should be discovering the hidden talents in the Church and releasing and guiding the inspiration and energies that people possess. They should be champions of freedom, and make sure that other people's initiative is encouraged and not quenched.

Essentially they are co-ordinators and initiators, but they do not interfere and thus stifle initiative in others. Leaders will also have the capacity to resolve the inevitable tensions and conflicts which arise in any community. They therefore need to take care that there are no such tensions between themselves, and that when they arise, they know how to deal quickly with them. As we begin to see the "every-member-ministry" principle adopted, the need for good leadership increases. The same is true if collegial leadership is to work properly. It needs careful handling, and the larger a church grows the more demands are put on the leadership.

Another way of looking at leadership is to examine the role of the chairman of a committee. In spite of all the cynicism about committees, it would be difficult to see how anything effective can be achieved in terms of leadership without the kind of interaction that a committee provides. It is bad committees and ineffective chairmen who are the bane of those organisations which are unfortunate enough to have them. Problems arise when committees are too large to work dynamically, or when the members themselves are not suitable. Another inhibiting factor is any mistrust between the members. But a bad chairman will always have a serious effect on any group leadership. He must be a person who leads firmly, but does not monopolise the conversation. His function is to draw out contributions from people, especially the shy and reticent members. He must lead, but not appear obviously to do so. He is free to make his own contributions, and to intervene, especially if he thinks an important issue is at stake. He should be able to co-ordinate the discussion, summarise it and interpret the implications to those present. He is not just a rubber-stamper, nor does he steam-roller the debate to suit his own interests. He is not there simply to see that the procedural rules are kept.

One can see how this can be applied to leadership in the Church. It is not a matter of telling people what to do, or of seeing that one has one's own way, or of guarding certain principles. It is a ministry which needs its own *charisma*. It should be as unobtrusive as possible. Most people are almost unaware of the best leadership. It is not oppressive, nor does it crush the individual. It helps each person to be free to express himself and to be himself. It is a co-ordinating role. Juan Carlos Ortiz has a striking illustration of this in his book *Call to Discipleship*: 'The work of the pastor,' he writes, 'is not that of a watchman who takes care that no one robs the bricks as they keep piling up, but a stonemason who builds them into the edifice.'[3]

We need to look carefully at how leadership arises in the Church. It is, of course, a ministry which is both called by God and gifted by him. Leaders are gifts of God to the Body of Christ for its growing maturity. Leadership has come to mean one of two things. Either it is something that is imposed from above, or it is the democratically elected choice of the people. But *both* these attitudes to leadership are wrong. The former is too remote from the people of God, from whom leadership derives, and for whom it exists. The latter, which is very common in the modern Church, is too close to the wishes of the people and tends to leave out of account the divine factors in both choice and equipping. Leadership is for the people of God. Fundamentally God is their leader, for they belong to him and to no one else. But God does delegate his leadership to men, whom he calls and enables. Thus leadership should arise naturally and spontaneously from the living church situation. The important thing to notice here is that leadership comes "from the ranks", so to speak. Stephen Clark in his book *Unordained Elders and Renewal Communities* describes the way in which leadership arose in the great ascetic movement of the fourth century.[4]

It is a very natural development. Unordained elders did not appear within the ascetic movement in response to any theory. No one taught that unordained elders were needed, nor did anyone, either the bishops or those involved in the ascetic movement, create them as a matter of strategy. Rather they emerged naturally within a particular situation... Since the old leadership patterns of church life were not adequate to the new situation, new leadership patterns emerged naturally ('charismatically') that were essential for both the health of the new movement and its good order within the Church.

The difficulty, of course, is that it is one thing to talk about "natural development", and another thing to try to relate all this to our current situations which have had another pattern imposed upon them, and in which ministry is seen not as something arising naturally within a local church, but as something (usually one person) who comes from outside to be "the ministry". But suffice it to say that, given openness to change (and without that nothing will prosper anyway), there is no reason at all why the present patterns in our churches cannot be adapted to the new vision which is being given of a plurality of leadership arising from within the congregation.

As leadership emerges, men (and I would include women too) with the necessary calling, dedication and gifts will band together, and amongst them will be one person who will have the gift of being a chairman or leader amongst leaders. The most natural way of relating this to our present situation in most churches would be for the minister himself to be the "paterfamilias" — the kind of focus of unity for the other leaders, and for the church as a whole. No one without such gifts should be ordained in the Church. Alas, some are, and the system breaks down. But even when this does happen, if there is sensitive lay leadership, and willingness on the part of the minister himself, it can still work, and the stronger lay leadership can be supportive of the weaker man.

Who are the leaders?

It is, of course, of the utmost importance that the right people are chosen to be the leaders in the Church, and here fortunately the New Testament gives us helpful guide-lines. But we need to allow many of our basic Western pre-suppositions regarding leadership to be challenged. David

Sheppard does this in his book *Built as a City*.[5] He distinguishes, for example, between what he calls "instrumental" leadership and "expressive" leadership. He gives us an example:

> The secretary who makes sure that people know what is expected of them is an example of instrumental leadership. The man who can put into words the strong feelings of the group is an example of expressive leadership. We should not expect that both will always be found in the same individual. A more corporate view sets free varied gifts of leadership.

Before David Sheppard became a bishop he was the warden of the Mayflower Family Centre in Canning Town in London's East End. He discovered that leadership became "a synonym for responsibility".

We have already dealt with one pre-supposition in chapter 8, namely the ministry of women, and the prejudice against female leadership. In case of misunderstanding let it be emphasised that *we include women with men in the discussions in this chapter on leadership*.

In 1 Timothy 3:1-7 and Titus 1:6-9, Paul tells us what to look for when appointing elders in the Church. The key phrase comes in Titus 1:8 — "master of himself". The leader is to be a person who is self-disciplined. The logic is clear. If a person cannot control himself, how can he properly pastor others? In his charge to the Ephesian elders Paul urges them to 'take heed to *yourselves*, and to all the flock' (Acts 20:28). But the leader is also to be someone who is able to manage his own household well, keeping his children submissive and respectful in every way (1 Tim. 3:4). The logic is equally clear, 'For if a man does not know how to manage his own household, how can he care for God's church?' Paul asks (v. 5). He is to be "above reproach", with a stable home life. Because he is an "elder" he should be an older person — that is mature in years — and spiritually mature, for he is not to be 'a recent convert, or he may be puffed up with conceit and fall into the condemnation of the devil' (v. 6).

It is important to see where Paul puts the stress. It is not on personal gifts as such, but on the person himself, and the quality of his life. The first question to ask when considering a potential leader is, 'Is that person's personal life in good order?' There is no mention by Paul of spiritual gifts as a necessary qualification for Christian leadership. The maturity expected of leaders would also imply an absence of any serious psychological problems. A person who finds it hard to work with others, and to relate satisfactorily to people, will not generally make a good leader. If we think of team leadership as the norm, then this is all the more important. The first thing that Paul mentions about the elder is that his married life should be in proper order — 'the husband of one wife'. In 1 Corinthians Paul discusses sexual morality before spiritual gifts. Charismatic abilities do not in themselves qualify anyone for leadership in the Church.

It needs also to be stressed that leaders must be dedicated people, wholly committed to the Lord Jesus Christ and to one another. The team of leaders will find it necessary to meet frequently. They will have to give much time to their ministry of leadership. If, for various reasons, they cannot do this, then they should not be leaders in the Church. For example, it would be a great temptation to appoint someone who holds an important post of leadership in the secular world to a similar position as an elder in the local church. But it may well be that his secular work means that he is not able through any fault of his own to give much time to the church. The temptation should be resisted, and no one appointed to leadership unless he can give a reasonable amount of his time to it. Leadership in a growing church is no sinecure, nor is it to be used to confer honours on people. It carries with it great responsibilities and should not be undertaken lightly by anyone.

Clever people do not always have gifts of leadership, neither do the rich and influential. Experts in various fields may have useful gifts to share, but that does not in and of itself qualify such a person for the role of leadership. All are called to holiness, and some are more saintly than others. But saintliness on its own is no qualification.

There are three especially dangerous traps for the unwary. The first is to give the responsibility of leadership to someone because he has been faithful for some time. It is a kind of reward. We feel the person will be hurt if he is not invited to become a leader. But again faithfulness itself is not a qualification for leadership in the Church. The second trap is to think of leadership in terms of representation; we must, so the thinking goes, have someone to represent the young people, the old people, the choir, etc., irrespective of whether he has particular gifts of leadership. The third trap, and the one we are most easily ensnared by, is to be afraid of what people will think of us if we pass them over. The fear of hurting people, and, therefore, of including those who may be unsuitable, is a powerful temptation which needs to be resisted. Our duty is not to please people and make everyone happy, but to share leadership amongst those who are truly called and properly equipped by God. It is fatal to think in terms of letting everyone "have a go".

In his book *Why Priests?* Hans Küng gives an interesting list of what he calls "variables" so far as qualifications for leadership in the Christian Church are concerned.[6] It should not necessarily be full-time nor life-long. It should not be seen as a social position separate from the rest of mankind. It does not require a university training. It is not a "science". It does not require celibacy and it should not be exclusively masculine. For a Roman Catholic this is a very liberal approach. But we do need to be shaken out of our tragically stereotyped approach to Christian leadership.

How are the leaders called?

We have already seen the importance of not divorcing leadership either from Christ himself — for he is the head of the Church, and all legitimate leadership derives from him — or from the Church itself, for leadership exists, not for its own sake, but to serve the Church, from which, of course, it is raised up. When it comes to calling people to leadership, these two points are absolutely crucial. For, in the first instance, all leaders are called by Christ. He appoints them, and he anoints them with the Holy Spirit and gives them the necessary *charismata* for the role they are to undertake. We must not think of asking the Lord to recognise and bless those whom we have chosen. Far from it. It is we who are to recognise and bless those whom God has chosen. Paul is most insistent about his own call. He was an apostle 'not from men nor through man, but through Jesus Christ and God the Father' (Gal. 1:1). In saying this, we are safeguarding the position of Christ as head of the Church. No person has any right to usurp his authority. He chooses whom he chooses.

But at the same time we have to establish the integrity of the Church. The ministry is for the Church, and every leader is at the same time a member of the Body. If it is true that God, as Paul puts it, 'has appointed in the Church first apostles...' (1 Cor. 12:28), it is the duty of the Church to discover who these people are and to give them the necessary support and authorisation. A personal call is not enough. We can all be self-deceived. That personal call needs to be confirmed and ratified by the Church. We find Paul humbly submitting his ministry to the other apostles at Jerusalem, 'lest somehow I should be running or had run in vain' (Gal. 2:2). And when Paul went out from Antioch on his first evangelistic tour, it was both the Holy Spirit *and* the church which called him and sent him out. Thus the calling of leaders can be seen as a delicate interplay between the revelation of the will of God to a person and to the Church as a whole. The Church calls and ordains those whom God has himself first called and ordained.

But there is a third factor which needs to be added. The obvious question at this stage to ask is, how does one know that God has called a certain person and how can the Church be sure of it? The plain answer is — the Lord will provide the necessary *charisma* of leadership and *charismata* for the particular ministry a person may be called to. The spiritual ability will be given, and the signs will be evident to the whole church. *It is here that the Church today has made the greatest mistake, with the most tragic consequences.* It has assumed that one can send a person to theological college or seminary and train him to be a minister. It has tended to select people for ministry on the grounds of what they may one day become, rather than on the basis of what they already are and have in Christ. *Charisma* cannot be earned or learned. A person either has it or hasn't, and God alone bestows it. A good example of this is Samuel the prophet. We are told that when he was a young man 'all Israel...knew that Samuel was established as a prophet of the Lord' (1 Sam. 3:20). This is how all ministry in general and the ministry of leadership in particular should arise and be recognised in the Christian community. People begin to say to one another, 'So-and-so has the gifts of leadership, hasn't he?' No one can be sure of the particular gifts he has until he has been tested in the fire of experience. They then become obvious and conspicuous for all to see. If this principle were followed, it would involve a radical change in policy regarding the selection and training of men for ministry. *What we are saying, in a nutshell, is that the Church generally has put the cart before the horse. Men are trained so that they may become ministers rather than trained because they are ministers, who already possess and are exercising their charismatic gift in the Church and the world.* Their fellow members in the Church say, 'That person has such-and-such a ministry' rather than 'That person would make a good minister.'

We need to look at this more closely. Vincent Taylor in his commentary on St. Mark's Gospel writes about apostles, 'They were aware of an inner call of Christ. This call was unmistakably attested to by the Holy Spirit and recognised and confirmed by the Church.'[7] Arnold Bittlinger expands on this and sees four characteristics.[8] First, the calling of God; then, the setting apart by the congregation; thirdly, the acknowledgment by the Church as a whole; and fourthly, the confirmation of the call by signs. If this is true of apostles, it should also be true for other ministries. The signs are important. They are the indication that the Church has "got it right". This person has truly been called and equipped by God. In the case of the apostle, one of the signs was the gift of the working of miracles. But there were others too. As E. Käsemann has pointed out, 'The actual sign of the apostle is not seen in single incidents of power in action and in ecstatic experiences, but, rather, in the continuity of an outstanding ministry in the congregation, performed sensibly and with charity, in patience and weakness.'[9] But there is a whole variety of ministries necessary for the growth of the Body of Christ. And the chief reason why we should set someone apart for a particular ministry is that he has the particular gift that is needed. We do not say, 'We need another teacher; Jim is a good fellow; let's pray that God will give him that particular gift', or 'Let's send him to a study course on teaching', but, 'Jim has the *charisma* of teaching, let's set him apart for teaching.' After that he can be sent on courses and learn all he can about how to teach. But if he does not have the divine call on the one hand and evidence, however rudimentary, of the divine enabling on the other, then he will never be much use as a teacher in the Church.

Hans Küng writes trenchantly about this:[10]

A bishop can never replace the Spirit of Christ by merely laying on his hands, if the Spirit is absent; he can never simply commission for the work of leadership those who happen to suit him and who do what he wants. When all human calls have been heard, if the call of God is missing, despite all ordination ceremonies the shepherd will prove to be a hireling. And perhaps it is true to say that unfaithful pastors are as common as false prophets and teachers of lies.

This able Roman Catholic theologian brings out the point we have been labouring about the need for a divine charism as a prerequisite for the setting apart for ministry, particularly the ministry of leadership, rather than something which will (hopefully) be picked up somewhere on the journey from theological college to ordination.[11]

> A basic direct or indirect 'officialisation' of charism is contrary to the New Testament. *A priori*, the charism has no need to be legitimated by an ecclesial institution, as the New Testament shows. On the other hand there are institutions, and representatives of institutions, who are without anything charismatic...and where there is no trace of the liberating Spirit of Christ, despite all institutional claims, there is no genuine ministry and no true leadership. [Hans Küng then mentions the other side of the coin.] The man who has these gifts and uses them, on the other hand, is performing genuine service and leading, even when he possesses no institutional commission. Therefore, a charism can be vitally effective without the institution... The institution without charism is dead; only where there is Spirit is there life.

Of course, he is not in these passages denying the place of ordination in the Church, and the need for the official recognition of ministries. Later on he says of ordination that it should be viewed as a wholly *legitimate development* and not as an instance of degeneration from apostolic times. But what he is saying is that without the God-given gift and call, it will be in vain.

Training for the ministry

This does lead one to the whole question of training for the ministry. Here one has to grasp the nettle firmly, for the implications of what one has been saying point in the direction of a completely new look. It is often forgotten that theological colleges are a comparative novelty. They began to make their appearance about a century ago, and so the Church seems to have survived for many centuries without them. It is no accident that extreme professionalism amongst ministers coincided with their advent. The evidence shows that theological education, as at present conceived, only perpetuates most of the false distinctions we have been exposing, and is, for the most part, a waste of time and the Church's valuable resources in manpower and money. It is interesting to reflect that in the Third World, the churches which are growing fastest are those which have little or no training for their pastors. This is particularly true of the Pentecostals, a factor which has been brought out by Christian Lalive D'Epinay in his survey of the Chilean Pentecostal assemblies *Haven of the Masses*.[12] The Pentecostal Church in Sweden, which has shown considerable growth and maturity since it was founded at the start of the twentieth century, still has no theological college for the training of its pastors.

It needs to be made clear that these remarks are not a form of anti-intellectualism, nor anti-clericalism as such. One is not saying that Christian leaders should not be educated, nor that no place should be given to theological training. On the contrary, all the evidence points in the opposite direction. We need better educated and trained leadership. What it consti-tutes is a criticism of the present method of theological education in general and of the part that theological colleges play in it in particular.

We need to ask ourselves two questions. The first one is, what kind of leadership does the Church need? And the second is, how can the Church best train people for that kind of leadership? Now we have emphasised three points, which the Church today generally ignores. The first is the necessity for team leadership or plurality of eldership. The second is that elders really are the *elders* of the local church, old enough and mature enough to lead. The third is that leadership arises from the Church and is not imposed upon it from outside. Our present system of theological education does not gener-ally prepare men for that kind of leadership. They are withdrawn from their local churches and cooped up in an artificial atmosphere with many others doing the same thing. More often than not, they do not return to their own church anyway, but are imposed upon some other church which they probably know very little about. And many of these men have not begun to be "elders" in age or maturity. They have not yet been tested in the world or the Church, and it is virtually impossible to ascertain at such an early age whether they have the *charisma* of leadership, or whether they will be able to work with others in team leadership.

J. Andrew Kirk has summarised this admirably in his critique of theological education:

(a)   It is exclusivist and élitist. It is largely reserved for a small minority of special candidates... It maintains the present distorted position of 'professionals' and 'amateurs' and thwarts the all-round growth of local leadership and stimulus of the gifts already apparent in the church.

(b)   It is based on the unexamined premise that intellectual knowledge (*intellectus fidei*) is the prime requirement for future leadership ability... It promotes false criteria for leadership and prolongs the clerical/lay divide...

(c)   It adopts a largely theoretical framework for its task. This means that theological reflection is conceived in a dialectical relation to other theological reflection (historical theology), what Jose Miguez calls the process of 'theology begetting theology', or Canon Sidney Evans, 'chewing-the-cud theology', rather than theology arising out of the Church's actual commitment to its missionary task. A largely residential pattern of theological education is inimical to a more praxis-orientated theological reflection. Moreover, it prolongs a situation in which the effective leadership of the church is in the hands of those who have been taught more how to communicate timeless truth than think creatively out of real situations. This also maintains two breeds of Christian in the churches.

(d)   It is based on a crisis-point theory of training by giving the impression that successfully concluded exams are the end of a structured-learning process.

The kind of qualities of leadership envisaged by Paul in 1 Timothy and Titus are only ascertainable when a person has at least reached the age of thirty, has been resident for several years in the place where he is to become a leader, and has been engaged in some secular work. For example, he should have had experience in bringing up a family; he must not be a recent convert, and he should be well thought of by unbelievers, which implies, of course, that he has been long enough in the place to be known to them, and probably has worked alongside them as well. Thus leadership should arise from the local church, where it has been tested and found worthy.

With regard to theological education, there are, roughly speaking, four levels to cater for. First there are those who will eventually become theologians in the Church. Secondly, there are those who are more gifted than most, and will rise to the top of the woodpile in the course of time, eventually becoming the *pastor pastorum* of large local churches, or trans-local leadership such as that of a bishop. Thirdly, there will be the less gifted academically who, because they possess the *charisma* of leadership, become leaders or elders in the local congregation. Fourthly, there are the more simple-minded, who may well have a *charisma* of leadership and will, therefore, become elders in the local church.

The potential theologian will be picked up early on because his prowess will be established academically at an early date. Some will hold positions in universities or other educational establishments. Normally they should not be ordained, but remain laymen. They should belong to a local church or Christian community, so that their academic studies and output are earthed to the realities of the Church and world. This should prevent a "theological gap" between theory and practice. Such people would also staff the theological colleges.

The person at the second level may have theological abilities, but mainly he will have outstanding gifts of leadership. He may have received a theological education at

...ot studied theology, he should do so as
...oing either post-graduate work or a course
...e provided by the Open University or corres-
...ourses. In addition, theological colleges of the
...ould provide short-term courses for this kind of
...n. He will, of course, belong to a local church, and there
his gifts of leadership will be tested and established. He will,
in time, become an elder of the church, and so continue to
rise from within the church to whatever higher position he
should later occupy.

The less gifted person will probably, in terms of leadership,
never get beyond the local church, but will, as he matures,
become an elder, and perhaps later a *pastor pastorum* of the
local church. His theological training will mainly be in the
local church. But theological colleges and other Christian
centres should lay on regular short-term courses in a whole
range of theological and pastoral subjects. In addition, the
people at the second level will increasingly have more to give
than most and their gifts would be squandered if available
only to one local church; so these men will have much to
share with the larger church, and be able to help the less
gifted in terms of leadership qualities, let us remember, not
spiritual maturity. It is important to stress that the short-term
courses would be for ministers and laity together, and that
increasingly that kind of distinction will be removed. They
would be for leaders in the church and also for others who
have ministries, such as teaching or healing, but who are not
leaders as such. 'Why is it,' writes layman George Goyder,[13]

that the Church of England spends hundred of thousands
of pounds a year on training the clergy, but next to nothing
on training the laity?... The laity need training as well as
the clergy, and they should be trained as far as possible
together. It does not help in preparing the clergy for their
life-work to immure them in a theological college for two
or three years at their most impressionable age, to surround
them with clergy and to imbue them with a clericalised

version of the Church... A more imaginative policy for using the theological college as a place of joint training for the clergy with laity is needed if the Church is to recover its relevance to the world.

The advantages of this approach to leadership in the Church are enormous. It would save a lot of money, which could be better spent on training the laity as well as ministers. It would virtually eliminate the "drop-outs", that is men who are ordained but who for various reasons leave the ministry and return to secular work. Ordination would only be for those who have developed a stable and mature life and who are already displaying their gifts of leadership. It would eliminate those who may have shown some promise and might reasonably be expected to develop gifts of leadership, but who for various reasons never do. There are those in our Churches who have been ordained prematurely, but with this hope in mind, who remain virtually passengers for the rest of their ministerial lives. It would lessen and in the end eliminate altogether professionalism, and ensure that ministers and laity train and work together from start to finish. It would mean also that, where you have exceptionally gifted laity in churches with proven gifts of leadership, they could simply be ordained without a penny being spent on their training or on their salary, because they would continue their secular work. This might not be possible in large churches, which require a full-time ministry, but it would be so in many smaller churches.

One of the greatest advantages in this approach would be the continuity of local church leadership. If there is a plurality of leadership, there will not be the normal hiatus which occurs when the minister leaves a church, and there is a search for a replacement, who is then imported from somewhere else. Also, there is a much greater opportunity for the gifted people in the local church to make their contribution, and for those who have the *charisma* of leadership to have this tested and tried before it becomes officially recognised.

This is not to say that there are not some difficulties and snags in such an approach. There would be legal problems, for example, so far as the Church of England is concerned, particularly in ordaining a person and presenting him to a church living while he continued his secular work. The major problem, however, which would need to be faced and overcome, would be that the stronger churches would be producing an abundance of leadership, while the weaker ones would not, and inevitably there would be, unless this was guarded against, a "haves"and "have-nots" situation. As with the economic circumstances of the richer and poorer countries in the world, the churches which are richer in leadership will get even richer, and the poorer churches poorer still. But this is where the trans-local leadership should come in, with responsibility to see that the richer churches are sharing their gifts, including their gifted people, with the poorer churches. It is a good military principle to reinforce success, and church strategy should not be to spread its resources thinly and evenly. Rather the Church should reinforce those churches which are experiencing success, in order that they in their turn can help other churches to be renewed. It is particularly important to see that churches in industrial areas and in the inner-cities which tend to be neglected, are reinforced and supplied with proper resources so that they can build up their own indigenous leadership.

Ordination

What we have come to call "ordination" was something which slowly evolved from apostolic times onwards. We cannot say that it was instituted by Christ; like eldership, it was taken over from Judaism as a natural development, and became of increasing importance as the Church grew. There was much "toing and froing" in the Roman Empire, and Christians made full use of the excellent communications system and the *Pax Romana*, which meant that travelling was comparatively fast and safe. But the Church had to safeguard itself from false ministries, and the development of what we now call "ordination" was accelerated because of the need to authorise certain ministries and to distinguish between the true and the false.

But there is evidence in the New Testament that ordination was a very early practice. In Acts 6 we are told about the Seven who were appointed to an administrative task. After they had been chosen (by the congregation), they were set before the apostles, who 'prayed and laid their hands on them' (6:6).[14] In Acts 13 Barnabas and Saul had hands laid upon them before they were sent off by the church at Antioch, although that action has little to do with what we call ordination, for it seems to have been a commissioning for a particular task. In Acts 14:23 we are told that Paul and Barnabas appointed elders in every church and, after 'prayer and fasting', 'committed them to the Lord in whom they believed'. Although the laying on of hands is not specifically mentioned, the word translated "appointed" is the verb *cheirotoneo*, which in later ecclesiastical usage means 'the laying on of hands'.[15] Literally the word means 'to choose by the raising of hands', the normal method in Greek cities of selecting officials. But by biblical times the meaning of the term had degenerated. As Arnold Bittlinger points out, 'If anyone "voted" on the issue, it was only Paul and Barnabas, who conferred with each other and then cast a concluding vote!'[16] If it does not mean they raised their hands to vote, it could mean that the apostles lowered their hands and laid them on the new elders. But that we cannot be sure of.

The only really clear reference to ordination in the New Testament is 1 Timothy 4:14, when Timothy had hands laid on him. It is generally assumed (as the normal translation suggests) that it was the elders who laid hands on Timothy. But it can mean, as Jeremias has pointed out, arguing from Judaic parallels, 'when hands were laid upon you with the object of making you a presbyter'.[17]

Some scholars assert, in view of the paucity of references in the New Testament, that ordination as such was unknown to the apostles. Eduard Schweizer, for example, says that Paul did not know ordination and, quite deliberately, never prescribed any rite for it.[18] W. Telfer says much the same in his book *The Office of a Bishop*.[19] Although it is likely that the method of appointing elders, just like eldership itself, was taken over from Judaism, it is important to remember that the laying on of hands was *not* practised in Judaism at this time. J. Newman says that after the ordination of Joshua by Moses there was no record of the laying on of hands for ordination in Biblical times or in the Rabbinical age. He cites the first reference in 380 A.D. [20]

But what is clear in the New Testament, whatever else may be said about a rite of ordination as such, is that men were appointed to be elders and to other specific tasks. From the very beginning there were clearly designated offices. Men in whom certain qualifications and qualities of life were discernible were set apart and recognised by the Church. Whatever ordination has now become, this principal element remains, namely that in ordination the Church, represented by its leaders, recognises God's call to the person who is to be ordained and God's equipment in terms of a *charisma* of leadership with other *charismata* also, and authorises that person to be a leader and to minister as such to the local church, and to the wider Church if he happens to be a bishop or some such trans-local leader. There may well be a special blessing in the ordination as such, and new grace and even *charismata* given. But generally speaking ordination does not confer on a person special gifts of leadership. These ought already to have been apparent, and if there is no evidence of them before ordination, then the person ought not to be ordained. *Ordination is essentially a recognition of abilities already evidenced in the life of a person and the authorisation of that person to exercise his gifts in the Body of Christ.* For some people, then, no theological training as such is necessary. For them such training would be more of a hindrance than a help in their development as leaders. For others, such training could be helpful. But ordination should never be viewed as a kind of graduation day ceremony or passing-out parade.

For Hans Küng ordination 'represents a call to the service of leadership, addressed publicly to a believer, by means of which the Church sanctions the call from God'.[21] But we need to be careful to limit its use to those called to leadership in the Church. There is a danger, if we extend it to other forms of ministry (e.g. deacons or administrators), that we create a new form of clericalism. It is better to keep matters as simple and uncomplicated as possible. We need also to be careful not to talk about confirmation as 'the ordination of the laity'. In a general sense *all* God's people are called to be "ministers". But we need to preserve carefully the distinction that *some* are called to a special ministry of leadership, and ordination should be kept for that ministry.

14

The Only Evidence:
A Summary of arguments

Growth is the only evidence of life.   Cardinal Newman

There are some other evidences of life, but growth is the most important and reliable one. If something is growing, it's alive. God's people must be set free to grow. At the same time we must never forget that whatever men may do — some planting as pioneers, others nurturing what has been planted and has germinated — it is only God who "gives the growth". (1 Cor. 3:7).

In this book we are not arguing against professionals, that is people who are called to full-time Christian work or leadership. Indeed, when the Church begins to grow, the need for such people increases rather than diminishes. We are, however, pleading for much more flexibility. There will always be an important place for a full-time ordained ministry. But we do need to know more clearly what that ministry is for.

Change there must be, and both growth and lack of growth demand it. We must not acquiesce in the Queen's rule in *Alice through the Looking Glass*, 'Jam tomorrow and jam yesterday, but never jam today.'

Chapters 1 and 2
1. The Church is in the "growth business". It is intended to grow both numerically and in spiritual maturity.
2. Ministry is for building up the Body of Christ (Eph. 4:12).

Chapters 3 and 4

3. Ministry has five main spheres — apostolic, prophetic, evangelistic, pastoral and didactic.

4. A healthy church should have a balanced ministry, which should include all of these spheres of ministry.

Chapter 5

5. The motive of ministry should be to serve, not dominate, people.

Chapter 6

6. Ministry is dependent on the Holy Spirit for its inspiration and effectiveness. The gifts of the Holy Spirit are some of the tools which God provides for our ministry.

Chapter 7

7. Ministry exists for the Church, not the Church for ministry.

8. There are local church ministries and trans-local ministries.

Chapter 8

9. Men and women are to be partners in ministry.

Chapter 9

10. Ministry involves us in commitment, submission and the exercise of authority. But the overriding consideration should be the new commandment to love one another.

Chapter 10

11. The New Testament does not set out to be a blueprint to answer all our questions about the ministry. There are some firm guidelines, but for the most part we should expect to be guided by the same Spirit who guided them, though sometimes in quite different ways.

Chapters 11-13

12. Leadership is a ministry to the Church and a gift of the Holy Spirit.

Chapter 11

13. Normally in the New Testament there is a plurality of leadership in the local church, and trans-locally as well.

14. Leaders (or elders) should normally be older people.

15. The offices of elders (presbyters) and of bishops are one and the same in the New Testament.

Chapter 12

16. Episcopacy was a natural development from the apostolate, by which elders received a wider or trans-local ministry of leadership.

17. We are not to look for apostles today, except in the limited sense of people who may be sent to perform specific tasks in different areas of the Christian Church.

Chapter 13

18. Leadership is essential for the well-being of the Christian Church, and ordination should be retained as a sound way of setting such leaders apart and giving authority and acceptance to their ministries.

Notes

Notes

Chapter 1

1. World Dominion Press, 1960, p.8.
2. Ex. 1:9-10.
3. See article on "spaciousness" by John F. A. Sawyer in *Annual of the Swedish Theological Institute in Jerusalem,* Vol. 6 (1968), pp.20-34 and *Semantics in Biblical Research, New Methods of Defining Hebrew Words for Salvation* (S.C.M., 1972), by the same author. This corrects the view expressed by Michael Green in *The Meaning of Salvation* (Hodder & Stoughton, 1965), p.15f and pp.96-118, whom David Sheppard quotes in *Built as a City* (Hodder & Stoughton, 1974), p.331. What John Sawyer maintains is that the concept of "spaciousness" cannot be derived from the Hebrew word *Yesa'* , which is the one most frequently used to describe "salvation", but that there are other significant Hebrew words with this concept which are used in Old Testament language about salvation, and so 'there is no need to resort to faulty linguistics to find it there.' I am indebted to Tony Thiselton for pointing this out to me.
4. Ex. 3:8.
5. Ex. 18:13-27.
6. I am indebted for this idea to J. Andrew Kirk in a preparatory paper for the NEAC 1977 Congress. See also R. de Vaux, *Ancient Israel, its Life and Institutions.*
7. Acts 6:1,7.
8. Acts 2:47.
9. *Let My People Grow*! Urban Project Workpaper No 1, sponsored by the Archbishops' Council on Evangelism.
10. Op. cit. p.6.
11. Op. cit. p.5.

12. Blond & Briggs, 1973, p.27.
13. Hodder & Stoughton, 1976.

Chapter 2

1. According to the Oxford Dictionary the word comes from the old French word *lai*. It was used to refer to people who are not in holy orders. The first recorded use of the word in this sense was in 1541.
2. *Enough is Enough* (S.C.M., 1975).
3. Op. cit., p. 7.
4. For full report see International Review of Missions Oct. 1920, pp. 573-4. Quoted in *Spontaneous Expansion of the Church*, p. 9.
5. Good Reading Ltd., 1975.
6. Op. cit., p. 16.
7. Op. cit., p. 22.
8. *A Question of Conscience* (Hodder & Stoughton, 1967), pp. 141-2.
9. *Small is Beautiful*, pp. 31-2.
10. Op. cit., p. 29.
11. *St. Paul's Epistle to the Ephesians* (Macmillan, 1904), pp. 99, 182. Also *The Epistle of Paul to the Ephesians* (Tyndale, 1963) by the Revd. Francis Foulkes.
12. Penguin Modern Classics, 1925, p. 234.
13. *Built as a City* (Hodder & Stoughton, 1974), p. 295.
14. Gabriel Murphy F.S.C., *Charisma and Church Renewal* (Officium Libri Catholici, 1965).
15. C.M.S. Newsletter, January 1966.
16. Terry Eagleton, *New Blackfriars*, December 1965.
17. Hodder & Stoughton, 1966, p. 35.

Chapter 3

1. Hodder & Stoughton, 1969, p. 283.
2. *Why Priests?* (Fontana, 1972), p. 26.
3. Op. cit., p. 27.
4. Eph. 4:11, 12.
5. *Built as a City*, p. 298.
6. see especially ch. 2.
7. see especially Ezekiel 34.
8. Agreed Statement, paragraph 3.
9. Hodder & Stoughton, 1974, p. 10.
10. Gen. 1:28.; 2:15.
11. S.C.M., 1975, p. 30.
12. Op. cit., p. 55.
13. *Fire upon the Earth* (Edinburgh House Press, 1958), p. 79.
14. 1 Sam. 3:1.
15. Hodder & Stoughton, 1970, p. 200.

16. Exod. 4:16.
17. *Charismen and Aemter in der Urkirche*, 1951, p. 117.
19. *Church Order in the New Testament*, footnote 750. For discussion of this point, see Arnold Bittlinger, *Gifts and Ministries*, pp. 53-4.
20. Matt. 28:19.
21. Acts 5:42.
22. 1 Tim. 3:2.
23. 1 Tim. 4:11, 1 Tim. 6:2, 2 Tim. 2:2.

Chapter 4

1. *Readings in St. John's Gospel* (Macmillan, 1945).
2. *A Church by Daylight* (Geoffrey Chapman, 1973), p. 211.
3. Op. cit., p. 302.

Chapter 5

1. *Church Order in the New Testament* (S.C.M., 1961), 21a-b.
2. *Why Priests?* p. 26.
3. *Ministers of God* (I.V.P., 1964), p. 35.
4. Section 7.
5. *The Future of the Christian Church* (S.C.M., 1971), p. 29.
6. *By What Authority?* (Darton, Longman & Todd, 1974), p. 132.
7. *The Church's Ministry* (Hodder & Stoughton), p. 27.
8. *The Pioneer Ministry* (S.C.M., 1961), p. 100.
9. *The Christology of the New Testament* (S.C.M.), p. 161.
10. Hodder & Stoughton, p. 13.
11. See Prof. Jeremias, *The Servant of God* (S.C.M.) quoted by Michael Green, *Called to Serve,* p. 14 (footnote).
12. *Life Together,* pp. 69-70.
13. *Readings in St. John's Gospel*, p. 210.
14. *Christ the Liberator* (Hodder & Stoughton, 1972), p. 22.
15. *The Preacher's Portrait* (Tyndale Press), 1961, p. 91.
16. *I will be called John* (Collins, 1974), p. 267.
17. *Called to Serve,* p. 51.
18. *Council Speeches of Vatican II* (Sheed & Ward, 1964), p. 69.
19. *Called to Serve,* p. 53.
20. Paternoster Press, 1959, pp. 42-3.
21. *Life Together*, p. 85.

Chapter 6

1. December 1st, 1975.
2. S.C.M., 1975, p. 88.
3. As H. Windisch, quoted by Dunn, p. 88.
4. Op. cit., p. 89.
5. Op. cit., p. 90.

6. Op. cit., p. 90.
7. Op. cit., p. 194.
8. Op. cit., p. 195.
9. Op. cit., pp. 87-8.
10. Op. cit., p. 359.
11. Op. cit., p. 360.
12. Murphy, pp. 105-7. He describes this intervention as a "momentous contribution".
13. Op. cit., p. 143.
14. Sections 5 and 8.
15. Darton, Longman & Todd, 1975, p. 9.
16. *A New Pentecost?* (Darton, Longman & Todd, 1975), p. 4.

Chapter 7

1. Section 7.
2. *The Future of the Christian Church*, p. 84.
3. Op. cit., p. 84.
4. The arguments for and against Pauline authority are laid out in Francis Foulkes, *The Epistle of Paul to the Ephesians* (Tyndale, 1963), p. 30f. The author cites several scriptural references from the earlier epistles of Paul showing that the concept of the universal Church was not entirely foreign to him. See, for instance, 1 Cor. 15:9, Gal. 1:13, and Phil. 3:6, and notably 1 Cor. 12.
5. Op. cit., p. 78.
6. *Call to Discipleship* (Good Reading Ltd., 1975), p. 95.
7. Op. cit., p. 94.

Chapter 8

1. Quoted by Father Jean Danielov. *The Ministry of Women in the Early Church* (The Faith Press, 1961).
2. February, 6th 1976.
3. *The Feminine* (Evanston, 1971), pp. 156, 164. Quoted in essay by John MacQuarrie in *The Way* (Summer 1975). This essay 'God and the Feminine' I found enormously helpful.
4. *1 Corinthians*, (Tyndale, 1958), p. 201.
5. *Commentary on 1 Corinthians*, (Saint Andrew Press, 1956).
6. S.C.M., 1969.
7. p. 359.
8. *Evangelism in the Early Church*, p. 118.
9. Quoted in *The Ordination of Women to the Priesthood*, a consultative document presented by thee Advisory Counil for the Church's Ministry, p. 33. This is a useful document, giving a summary of the various arguments for and against the ordination of women.
10. Cyril Barnes, *The Words of William Booth* (Salvation Army, 1975), p. 14.

11. *My Best Men are Women* (Hodder & Stoughton, 1974), p. 17.
12. R. Collier, *The General next to God* (Collins, 1965), p. 42.
13. See *The Ordination of Women to the Priesthood*, p. 41, para. 167.
14. Article 'God and the feminine', *The Way*, Supplement No. 25, p. 7.
15. Op. cit. p. 8.
16. *Inner and Outer Space: Reflections on Womanhood* in *The Woman in America*, ed. R. J. Lifton (Boston, 1965), quoted by MacQuarrie, pp. 8-9.
17. 'Human nature and the Fall: A Psychological View', in *Man, Fallen and Free*, ed. E. Kemp (London, 1969), p. 54.
18. December 11th, 1971.
19. *Theology*, September 1954.
20. *Evangelicals and the Ordination of Women*, Grove Booklet, 1973, p. 24.
21. *Women and Holy Orders*, 1966, p. 126.
22. Op. cit., p. 26.

Chapter 9
1. *By What Authority?* (Darton, Longman & Todd, 1974), p. 111.
2. *Built as a City*, p. 333.
3. *In God's Underground*, (W. H. Allen, 1968), p. 170.
4. January 1976.
5. Inter-Varsity Press, 1975, p. 140.
6. Op. cit., p. 142.
7. Rom. 15:26 (the collection for the poor of Jerusalem), also 2 Cor. 8:4, 2 Cor. 9:13, Phil. 4:15, 16. It is also implied in 1 Tim. 6:18 and Heb. 13:16. It is probably in mind too in Gal. 6:6, Phil. 1:5, Philem. 6:17.
8. *Unordained Elders and Renewal Communities* (Paulist Press, 1976), pp. 18-19.
9. *Contra oppugnatores vitae monasticae III*, 14.
10. Hodder & Stoughton, 1973.
11. Op. cit., p. 84.
12. *Discipleship* (Marshall, Morgan & Scott), 1976.
13. *Call to Discipleship* (Good Reading, 1975). This is very similar to the above book, p. 67.
14. Op. cit., pp. 77-8.
15. *Brethren, Hang Loose* (Zondervan, 1972), pp. 173-4.
16. Fontana, 1972, pp. 85-6.
17. *Life Together*, p. 85.
18. See especially pp. 291-7 and Conclusions 50.2-50.3.
19. Op. cit., p. 292.
20. Op. cit., p. 299.
21. Op. cit., p. 81.

Chapter 10
1. Coverdale, 1973, pp. 141-2.

Introduction to Part III

1. See his conclusions, p. 345f.
2. Op. cit., p. 349.

Chapter 11

1. See the dissertation on the Christian Ministry in Bp. Lightfoot's commentary on Philippians. Also Leon Morris *Ministers of God* (IVP, 1964), pp. 72-5, and William Barclay *By What Authority?* (Darton, Longman & Todd, 1974) pp. 134-5.
2. *Called to Serve* pp. 39-40.
3. J.T.S. No. XXV Vol. 2.
4. *By What Authority?* p. 137.
5. *The Body of Christ* (Hodder & Stoughton, 1964), p. 42.
6. See Michael Green, *Called to Serve*, pp. 19-20.
7. *Agreement on the Doctrine of the Ministry* (Grove Books 1973), p. 21. This is further endorsed by one of the Roman Catholic participants in this International Commission, Jean M.R. Tillard. He writes, 'Nowhere does Scripture tell us in a precise way who presides at the eucharist: nowhere does it show one of the Twelve or one of the ministers of which it speaks carrying out this task. There is no evidence to justify our affirming that presiding at the Holy Banquet was necessarily closely connected with one or other of the ministerial functions attested in the apostolic writings' *What Priesthood has the Ministry?* (Grove Books) (no. 13) 1973. A reprinted paper commissioned by the Anglican/Roman Catholic International Commission.
8. Op. cit. p. 7, para. 12.
9. Op. cit. p. 29.
10. 152f. As also in my own church of Holy Trinity, Hounslow.
11. Paulist Press.
12. Quoted by Stephen Clark, p. 39.
13. *Ministers of God*, p. 90.

Chapter 12

1. *Bishops in the Church*, (Church Book Room Press, 1966), p. 13.
2. *Charisms and Church Renewal*, p. 101.
3. In a series of studies *Gemeinde und Gemeindeordnung* culminating in *Church Order*, quoted by Dunn, p. 272.
4. See his essay on 'Ministry and Community' in *Essays on N.T. Themes*, quoted by Dunn, p. 272.
5. *The Church*, p. 179ff.
6. *The Gospel According to Mark* (1959), p. 626ff. Michael Green believes that this explanation by Dr Vincent Taylor is open to criticism and is based on some questionable exegesis.
7. *Jesus and the Spirit*, p. 273.

8. *Theology of the New Testament* (S.C.M., 1952), p. 60.
9. Op. cit., p. 274.
10. *Church Order in New Testament* (S.C.M., 1961), p. 30.
11. Op. cit., p. 24b.
12. See Gordon Strachan, *The Pentecostal Theology of Edward Irving* (Darton, Longman & Todd). Dr. Reiner-Friedemann Edel, *Heinrich Thiersch als oekumenische Gestalt,* (Marburg, 1962).
13. See Bethany Fellowship, 1972, p. 15.
14. *Edward Irving and his Circle* (James Clarke, 1934).
15. Larry Christenson, op. cit., p. 48.
16. For a study of the Apostolic Church see W. A. C. Rowe, *One Lord One Faith* (Puritan Press); Hugh Dawson and others *Tenets of the Apostolic Church*; William Henry Lewis, *And He gave some Apostles.*
17. Op. cit., p. 168. This is similar to a part of James Dunn's thesis in his book *Jesus and the Spirit.*
18. *The Early Church,* (S.C.M., 1956), p. 78.
19. *Christianity Divided,* (Sheed & Ward, 1961), p. 10.
20. *Galatians*, p. 194.
21. *William Temple, his Life and Letters* (O.U.P., 1948), p. XII.
22. *Growing into Unity* (London, 1970), p. 77.
23. *Bishops in the Church*, p. 13.
24. Polyc. 1.
25. *Evangelism in the Early Church,* p. 170.
26. E.g. the Bishop of Colorado lives in a community household with 16 others.

Chapter 13

1. *Why Priests*? p. 61.
2. Op. cit., p. 62.
3. Op. cit., p. 29.
4. Op. cit., p. 48.
5. pp. 286-7.
6. Op. cit., p. 54.
7. *The Gospel according to St. Mark*, p. 626ff.
8. *Gifts and Ministries*, p. 58f.
9. 'Die Legitinitat des Apostles', *Zeitschrift fur die neutestamentliche Wissenschaft* (1942), p. 68.
10. Op. cit., p. 63.
11. Op. cit., p. 65.
12. Lutterworth, 1969.
13. *The People's Church*, pp. 35, 56-7.
14. It does not actually say that the apostles laid their hands on them and it could have been the church, which had selected them. But the strong inference is that it was the apostles, for why else were they set before them? It would have been a most clumsy affair if the church had performed the laying-on of hands.

15. e.g. In the Didache (15:1) the word is used for the choice
     of bishops and deacons.
16. *Gifts and Ministries*, p. 36.
17. *The New Testament and Rabbinic Judaism* (London, 1956), p. 244ff.
18. *Church Order in the New Testament*, p. 25b.
19. Darton, Longman and Todd, 1962, p. 41f.
20. *Semikhah* (M.U.P., 1950), p. 102.
21. Op. cit., p. 67.

Bibliography

Bibliography

This is by no means a comprehensive list, but includes those which the author has relied on most fully.

1. *General books on the ministry*

John P. Baker (editor)	*Christ's Living Body*	Coverdale, 1973.
Arnold Bittlinger	*Gifts and Ministries*	Hodder & Stoughton, 1974.
James D. G. Dunn	*Jesus and the Spirit*	S.C.M., 1975.
Michael Green	*Called to Serve*	Hodder & Stoughton, 1964.
Hans Küng	*Why Priests?*	Fontana, 1972.
Leon Morris	*Ministers of God*	I.V.F., 1964.
Eduard Schweizer	*Church Order in the New Testament*	S.C.M., 1961.

2. *Dynamic appraisals of the ministry*

Robert Girard	*Brethren, hang loose*	Zondervan, 1972.
Juan Carlos Ortiz	*Call to Discipleship*	Good Reading, 1975.
Leslie Paul	*A Church by Daylight*	Geoffrey Chapman, 1973.
David Sheppard	*Built as a City*	Hodder & Stoughton, 1974.
Howard Snyder	*The Problem of Wineskins*	I.V.P. (U.S.A.), 1975.
Ray Steadman	*The Church comes alive*	Regal, 1972.

3. *The ministry of women*

Colin Craston (editor)	*Evangelicals and the Ordination of Women*	Grove, 1973.
Report to General Synod	*Ordination of Women to Priesthood*	1972
John Macquarrie	God and the Feminine	*The Way* (Supplement 25), 1975.

4. *The ministry of the Holy Spirit*

Roland Allen	*The Spontaneous Expansion of the Church*	World Dominion Press, 1960.
Roland Allen	*The Ministry of the Spirit*	World Dominion Press, 1960.
Gabriel Murphy	*Charisms and Church Renewal*	Catholic Book Agency, 1965.
Cardinal Suenens	*A New Pentecost?*	Darton, Longman & Todd, 1975.

5. *Reports*
Let my people Grow and *Divide and Conquer* Workpapers
(Sponsored by the Archbishops' Council on Evangelism).

Julian W. Charley	*Agreement on the Doctrine of the Ministry*	Grove, 1973.

6. *"Apostolic" Churches*

Larry Christenson	*A message to the Charismatic Movement*	Bethany, 1972.
A.L.Drummond	*Edward Irving and His Circle*	James Clarke, 1934.
Hugh Dawson etc.	*Tenets of the Apostolic Church*	(privately published)
W. A. C. Rowe	*One Lord, One Faith*	Puritan Press.

Index

Index

Authors of books, from which quotations have been taken, are in italics. Where a subject has been dealt with in greater detail, the page numbers are in bold type.